The Devil's Scourge

THE
DEVIL'S
SCOURGE

Exorcism During the Italian Renaissance

GIR⊙LAM⊙ MENGHI

Translation, Introduction, and Commentary by GAETAN⊙ PAXIA

WEISERBOOKS
Boston, MA/York Beach, ME

First published in 2002 by
Red Wheel/Weiser, LLC
York Beach, ME
With offices at:
368 Congress Street
Boston, MA 02210
www.redwheelweiser.com

Library of Congress Cataloging-in-Publication Data

Menghi, Girolamo, 1529–1609.
    [Selections. English. 2002]
    The devil's scourge: exorcism in Renaissance Italy / [compiled by]
    Gaetano Paxia; translated by Janet Sethre.
        p. cm.
    Includes bibliographical references.
    ISBN 1-57863-235-8 (alk. paper)—ISBN 1-57863-265-X (pbk. : alk.
    paper)
    1. Exorcism—Liturgy—Texts. 2. Catholic Church—Liturgy—Texts.
    I. Paxia, Gaetano, 1938-II. Title.
BX2340 .M4613 2001
265'.94—dc21

                                    2001046721

Typeset in 11.5 Sabon

Printed in Canada

TCP

09 08 07 06 05 04 03 02
 8 7 6 5 4 3 2 1

The paper used in this publication meets the minimum requirements of the
American National Standard for Information Sciences—Permanence of Paper for
Printed Library Materials Z39.48-1992 (R1997).

CONTENTS

PREFACE

This volume presents a translation of ancient texts used in exorcism, written in Latin and published for the first time in 1576 by the famous exorcist, Girolamo Menghi (1529–1609).

I hope it can contribute to a deeper understanding of the horrendous, mysterious world of demonic realities. St. John Chrysostom (345–407), while preaching about the "devil as tempter," began with these words, which I wish to adopt as my own: "We deal with these facts, not because we have pleasure in speaking of the devil, but so that you may understand with certainty the doctrine concerning him."[1]

An acquaintance with the world of the devil, and with the complex, fascinating rites of exorcism described here, can shed light on the history of Christianity, on humankind, and on sin and evil as viewed during the Renaissance. Today, some people speak of the "death of Satan." Many believe that devils are symbols, created or projected outside of ourselves, and that, therefore, it is useless to study them. Such research, they claim, can only reflect an obsolete mentality. And yet, interest in the "Prince of the Netherworld" is present today, and growing ever more lively. The cinema industry is caught up in the demonic world; newspapers are increasingly full of articles describing satanic rites and sects. We should, at any rate, ask what increases our interest in the world of the diabolical during certain periods of history. Is it the Church's need to affirm its power? Is it our wish to give a name to that which afflicts us in order to face it less traumatically?

Exorcists use liturgical prayers, gospel readings, invocations, and imprecations to carry on an implacable struggle against the demon who has taken possession of a subject's body. The devil is attacked as if it were a ferocious beast whose freedom of action must be bridled. Its presence is seen as a surfeit of evil, a horrendous contamination of God's creature, a horrible tragedy, a test that is mysterious and frightening for the person undergoing it.

Exorcists are caught up in the drama being played out inside the body of a person redeemed by Christ, but now dominated by the "Prince of Lies." They try to heal the victim through long, extenuated prayers taken partly from very ancient texts; through imprecations that often reach the point of violence; and through imperious, nearly desperate urgings.

Here and there, we see highly contrived, melodramatic forms. A lively, prolonged duel, or duet, takes place. Sometimes you can almost smell the fire and brimstone to which the devil's presence is repeatedly condemned. One always expects the devil to respond to the exorcist's words of damnation in a cavernous, corrupted voice. One expects the devil to agree to leave that funereal abode of inquietude and death that the possessed person's body has become.

This investigation of the world of demonology concentrates primarily on the period of the Italian Renaissance and the Reformation. Society was then attempting to free itself from the Church's pretense of being the only source of truth. People wanted to define their own personal, autonomous relationship with God. On one hand, Menghi's exorcisms express the author's sincere conviction of the need to drive the devil's evil presence out of society. On the other, they are perhaps an attempt to give new energy and spectacular force to the Catholic Church, which, at that moment, was undergoing a process of political and religious reshaping.

Devil, evil, sin. If we leaf through theology books, we note that many theologians today do not believe in Satan, or in devils as personal, individual beings. Suffice it to recall the American theologian Henry A. Kelly or Herbert Haag of the University of Tubingen, who has written three books to demonstrate the non-existence of the devil. Does the devil exist? Does the devil incarnate evil or the Evil One? In the opinion of some, anyone can perform an evil, diabolical function. When Peter acts to block the mission of Christ by physically defending him, Christ says: "Get behind me, Satan! You are an obstacle in my path, because you are thinking not as God thinks but as human beings do" (Matt. 16:21–23). Theologian Giovanni Franzoni notes that even our brother may exercise a diabolical function, if he sets up an obstacle in our path toward God.[2]

I like to imagine the devil as a lonely, sad being who, ever more desperate, is abandoned to an assigned role of an ugly, black bird—stoned down, or lost in a gray sky, inquisitor or guilty sinner, incapable of showing any penitence. I see the devil as a sad beast, a sick wanderer who drifts here and there, toward a time and place that ultimately bring peace and—who knows—forgiveness. But perhaps this is an excessively romantic vision to have of one who is held to be our most cruel adversary.

An ancient prayer of the early Church, written by St. Ignatius of Antioch (d. 107), describes the devil as one bent on leading the redeemed away from God, while the redeemed are willing even to accept martyrdom, just to remain by the side of Christ:

Let no creature, visible or invisible, draw me to him, so that I may be of Jesus Christ. Though fire and cross befall me, and herds of beasts, lacerations, dismemberment, fracturing of bones, amputations of body parts, complete slaughter of the body, tremendous torments of the devil, may I be of God.[3]

PART I

Demonology:
A Historical Perspective

1

DEMONOLOGY FROM ANTIQUITY
TO THE RENAISSANCE

Devil, evil, sin. These words keep reappearing in our thoughts, our speech, our readings, our experience. They are connected by a kinship of meaning that often evades definition, although clearly each denotes a moral disorder or spiritual inquietude in our existence. How many times have you used the expression, "That man is a devil" to indicate that someone has reached a certain level of degradation or perversion? How many times have you used the term "devilish" ambiguously, to describe a being or situation that threatened to entice your spirit to revolt?

These words exert a certain power over us through their connection, albeit apposite, to another word: God. Through a primitive thought process, the devil, evil, and sin have become natural antitheses to the concept of God.

Satan somehow gives us the idea that we are endowed by implication with craftiness, with an aggressive, disintegrative force—a supernatural, almost divine power sometimes accompanied by a sense of horror or fear. Traditional religion encourages us to impute the very roots of evil to Satan: sin, deceit, falsity, unexpected betrayal in our love relationships. Everything that torments us in a mysterious, disquieting way, everything diabolical or demoniacal, is defined as satanic. Indeed, our culture has grown accustomed to the idea of the devil as a disturbed, solitary presence: both individual and multiple; endowed with will, but perverse; gifted with superior intelligence, but bent on deceit. As a result, our interest in this hidden, invisible being—full as he is of potential existential threat, is reduced.

A lengthy discussion of popular demonology is beyond the scope of this work. This phenomenon includes elements from Christian theology as well as pre-Christian paganism. Of course, the common people see the devil as a powerful being, endowed with almost divine strength, and having a nearly infinite capacity for metamorphosis. The capacity to evoke the devil is attributed in particular to women—witches—who, invaded by the spirit of evil, can perform evil spells of all kinds.[1] We will, however, begin with a brief look at some examples of demonic lore from various ancient, theological, and scholastic traditions.

The Devil in the Ancient World

In primitive cultures, the evil characteristics of demons were not always fully articulated. The negative characterization tends to become more firmly entrenched in more advanced civilizations. In the Mesopotamian culture, the people harbored an active terror of demons. In reality, however, these demons were not so much devils as souls of the dead who were said to return to Earth to torment the living, with whom they had debts to settle. Today, there remain fragments of exorcisms against some of these demons: the Utukku demons, who hid out in the desert; Lamashtu, a she-devil; and Labartu, another she-devil who was said to haunt children.

There were demonic figures in ancient Egypt as well, for example, Apopi, the great serpent, a bitter enemy of Osiris-Ra. Ammit is mentioned in the *Book of the Dead*: a monstrous being that devours the dead who have been condemned by Osiris. In later periods of Egyptian history, belief in demons grew. People spoke of demons that caused disease, madness, and other ills.

Hindu tradition also identifies groups of diabolical beings: the Asura, hostile to the gods; the Bhuta, enemies of humankind; the Raksasa, who hinder the performance of rites; and the Pisaka, horrid beings who feed on human flesh. Nor does Buddhism avoid mentioning demons, seen as fragile entities, subject—like people—to the negative circuits of existence, to pain, and to death, from which they try to free themselves by following the light of Buddha. The most potent Buddhist demon is Mara, who tries to hinder the Enlightened One in his mission. The Tibetan tradition presents demons as adversaries of Lamaism who provoke great evils and spread horrendous diseases. In the Chinese tradition, demons such as Sha and Kuei prefer to operate at night, bringing evil to the unfortunate. Greek mythology, of course, had its evil demons as well, including Eurinomos, the demon who fed on the flesh of cadavers, and Empusa, a nocturnal demon that also nourished itself on rotting flesh. Lamia was said to devour children and to take out its eyes at night in order to sleep. The Greeks, however, held that some demons inspired people to act for the good. Finally, although I don't have time to enumerate them here, the great monotheistic religions such as Judaism and Islam also had their respective pantheons of demonic figures.

The Devil in Early Christianity

In Western cultures, it is mainly the Christian theological tradition that has defined Satan—as the Tempter, imbued with carnality, and the enemy of ourselves and Christ.

Preachers in Christian communities have always presented
the devil in horrid, fantastic visions, as the ambassador of
all spiritual desperation, so that the faithful would move
away from evil and moral disorder. The devil is seen by
Christians as the incarnation of revolt against God.

During the earliest period of Christian history, in the
"apostolic and apologetic tradition," God was presented as
the Savior, while the devil was the bearer of disorder. Yet
Christians had to insist on one God, the Creator, in order
to avoid falling into polytheism or Manicheism, which
threatened to become widespread among Christians during
the 4th and 5th centuries. St. Augustine himself belonged to
the sect for a time, before his conversion. Founded by
Mani, a Persian from Mesopotamia who lived during the
3rd century, Manicheism taught that there were two equally
eternal and uncreated principles: the principle of light, of
the truth that is God, and the principle of darkness and lies,
or the devil. The devil is bound to do evil, to spread evil.
According to the Manichees, the devil is, in fact, the incarnation of an irrational, empty, purposeless, and brutal evil.
When he abandoned Manicheism, St. Augustine claimed
that the devil had once been a good angel; that "everything
was created good by a supremely good Creator"
(*Confessions*, 7, 3, 5). True, he argues, there exists a contrast between God and the devil, just as there is contrast
between love and hate, good and evil. The devil, however,
is not an omnipotent evil, but rather a creature of God who
has freely chosen to dedicate himself to evil.

The Councils of Nicea (325 A.D.) and Constantinople
(382 A.D.) insisted on God as the creator of all things "visible and invisible." St. Ireneus, born around 135–140 A.D.,
insists that the devil betrayed God's expectations by going
away from the good to which he had been destined. God
was thus obliged to drive him out of heaven and consign
him to the eternal fires of hell. The devil, claiming he had a
right to power and grace by his very nature, took revenge

by urging Adam and Eve to sin. Stubbornly, he rebelled against God, hindering the path of mankind, who was then spiritually saved by the sacrifice of Christ.[2]

The African Tertullian, born at Carthage around 160 A.D., was an erudite scholar, knowledgeable in Roman law. In writing a treatise against Marcione, he insists on the unity of God, and on God's identity with the Creator. The devil, he claims, was created by God as a marvelous, luminous creature who, in an exercise of free will, decided to contravene God.[3] In another work, the struggle against the devil and his works is presented as one of the main reasons for Jesus' incarnation: "The Son of God has come in order to destroy the works of the devil."[4] Baptism is presented in the New Testament as an ingenuous, sweet ritual compared to the Old Testament passage of the Red Sea: the believer is saved through the grace of baptism, and the devil, seen as the pharaoh, drowns.[5] We find this image in Origen as well.[6]

St. Cyprian, Bishop of Carthage, who was martyred in 258 A.D., informs us that the devil was created as a "great angel of majesty," but that he then degraded himself, becoming the first sinner, deceiving the minds of humans, driving them to division and doctrinal distortions, and separating them from the true faith.[7] From that point on, the entire life of the Christian believer became a struggle against Satan and his temptations. Only with humility, and through the gift of God's grace, can one win out against him.[8]

St. Clement of Alexandria (150–215 A.D.) emphasizes the fundamental importance of the human will in our actions. He urges us not to fear the devil, since we sin only when consciously choosing evil. Evil, he points out, is just a false and empty illusion of the true and lasting good.[9] Through his redemption, Christ, who became a man and suffered till death, destroyed the dominion of evil and of death itself. He pointed the way to salvation for humankind through baptism. We can win out over the diabolical influences that drive us to spiritual shipwreck; we can preserve our new life in Christ.[10]

Origen (185–254 A.D.), the most famous disciple of Clement of Alexandria and one of the early Church's most learned men, held that the devil is not bad by nature, because if he were, he would not be responsible for anything. One who is bad by nature, he pointed out, cannot do anything but evil, and so cannot be held guilty or accountable.[11] True, the devil chooses evil, but he is a creature of God, even when he tempts us toward evil. Like us, he does not cease being a creature of God, even when he sins. Origen's Satan acts out a miserable role, eternally condemned to self-destruction, approaching a state of nonbeing as a result of his opposition to God.[12]

Origen's view of the eternity of hell is famous. He believes that, at the end of time, there will be a universal reconciliation, and that, therefore, even the devil will be saved.[13] This is the so-called *apocatastasis*, or reconciliation between God and all creation, including Satan and death. This doctrine was accepted by several fathers of the Eastern Church, among them St. Gregory Nissene, and by several theologians, such as Scotus Eriugena. The true evil of the devil lies in the fact that he, an angelic creature, chose to dedicate himself to evil, giving rise to evil in the world.

Lactantius (260–330 A.D.) asks what can explain the mysterious presence of evil and the devil in the world. He answers that evil exists in order to foster good. If there were not both evil and good, there would be no possibility of choice, and thus no freedom. "We could not perceive virtue if there were not the opposite vice; nor could we use virtue if we were not tempted by its opposite."[14]

Eusebius of Caesarea (4th century) believed that, in rebelling against God by choice and with guilt, the devil was forced to lose his enormous, splendid, divine virtues, and to identify himself with evil.[15] Athanasius, Bishop of

Alexandria (328–372 A.D.), confronts the problem of where the devil lives, now that he has fallen from heaven. The devil lives in the air, he says, like a bird drifting between heaven and Earth. From the air, he tries to hinder man in his path toward God.[16]

Other Church Fathers seem to hold the same opinion, including St. John Chrysostom (345–407 A.D.).[17] Chrysostom also asks what was the devil's original sin. He categorically states that it certainly was not the union with woman—not a sin of lust—for the simple reason that women did not yet exist. Sin, in fact, occurred before the creation of man. He maintains that it was a sin of arrogance and vanity,[18] while St. Ambrose, Bishop of Milan from 374 to 397 A.D., claims that the devil was prompted by envy of the destiny of humans, who had obtained what the devil, himself, had lost—grace.[19]

St. Augustine, himself, believed that demons were condemned to live in the air like dry leaves, and had a body made of air that obviously could not be corrupted. They were, however, subject to torments.[20] In his sermons, when speaking about the snares of the devil, the saint from Ippona attributes great importance to human responsibility. Sin exists, he clearly states, only when people of action can say: "It was I."[21] And we must remember that, though they can harm us, Satan's actions are devoid of force if we adhere to Christ.[22]

In the view of Cassian, Bishop of Marseilles around the year 400, there are demons who *specialize* in different types of temptations and vices; cruel demons, clownish demons, libidinous demons, etc.[23] St. Gregory the Great (540–604 A.D.) says that devils and evil, perverse persons constitute a unity, a kind of mysterious body of sin: "*Unum corpus sunt diabolus et iniqui.*"[24] St. Isidor, Bishop of Seville (560–636 A.D.), believed that God used the devil to scourge and humiliate mankind when he found it useful.[25] St. Maximus, monk and hermit (580–662 A.D.), adds that the diabolical temptation can be transformed into a moment of Christian growth, of spiritual fortification and perfection. At such moments, we can perceive our frailty and so our need of God's help.[26]

St. John Damascene (675–749 A.D.) bitterly remarks in *De fide orthodoxa* that the devil was created as light and chose darkness; he was the nearest creature to the Good, elevated to a supreme spiritual life, but became the lack of light and good.[27] God wanted to leave him free, even if that freedom allowed him to choose to oppose God himself.

The Devil in Scholastic Thought and Literature

During the centuries of scholastic theology, demonology was widely discussed, even on a philosophical level. In his comment on St. Paul's *Letter to the Ephesians*, St. Bruno (1035–1101 a.d.) says that the power of devils has been restricted to the air, where they live by divine command. If they lived on Earth, notes the saint, the fruits of the Earth would be spoiled.[28] It is the elect who will judge the devil, Bruno adds, asking them to account for their works. Believers will ask why they did not pursue the good, and why they caused so much evil to poor human creatures.[29]

According to Hildebert of Le Mans, men were created in order to replace the fallen angels, so that God could be freed of a mysterious loneliness.[30] Brunone of Asti (1042–1123 A.D.) observes that the struggle between the devil and woman, spoken of in the Apocalypse, should be read as an ecclesiastical key. The woman spoken of is the Church, who will undergo constant moral stress caused by the devil. Brunone calls Satan "Bechemot" (beast),[31] and claims that, having abandoned his angelic dignity, the devil imitates the ferocious beasts, perennially condemning us to extreme anxiety in our lives.

The highly original view of Honoré of Autun emerges in the 12th century. Honoré believes that God certainly fore-saw the fall of the demons, but created them just the same, somewhat as an ornament to his creative work, analogous to a painters who need to spread black paint over their palettes in order to create the darker tones.[32] Rupert of Deutz (1070–1129) claims that the darkest abyss is reserved for Satan, though he was once a cherubim, all light and grace. Unfortunately, Rupert claims, the devil expected to be considered a god, a creator of angels; instead, he became the father of falsity.[33]

St. Anselm, Bishop of Canterbury from 1093 to 1109, notes that we were redeemed by Christ. In order to save the devils, however, Christ would have to "angelify" himself once for each fallen angel in order to save them.[34] Abelard (1079–1142) warns us to beware the devil's snares. The devil, he cautions, acts outside of the confines of divine permission.[35]

St. Thomas Aquinas (1221–1274) summed up the medieval tradition of demonology developed by other Christian theologians, such as Anselm of Aosta, and Pietro Lombardo, author of the *Sententiae*. Devils, Aquinas argues, were created as luminous angels, but were stained by the deep pride shown before their creator. Their perversity, which makes them personifications of evil, is not due to their nature, but to their precise, insistent will. Their opposition to God, to the supreme good, was a choice for which they showed no penitence. Many were the angels who separated themselves from God and became his opponents; many, however, remained faithful to God. After the fallen angels' separation from God, their deviant will remained perennially bound to evil, with no possibility for change. Their place of perdition is hell, where they torture the damned, and the air, from which they depart in order to approach us and tempt us to evil. Their true punishment is spiritual.[36] Clearly, the nature of devils as described by Thomas is not mixed with material elements; he affirms their full spirituality, since they are angelic beings. Their pain arises from everything that opposes their perverse will.

Their punishment, the "fire" so often mentioned, reaches them everywhere, because they are the source of it by virtue of their separation from God.[37] St. Thomas speaks of devils in several works (*Summa Theologiae, Comment on the Sententiae, Summa Contra Gentes*). His doctrine remained fundamentally unaltered during the Middle Ages and the Renaissance. After the Reformation, it was accepted by many non-Catholic theologians.

Contrary to what many believe, interest in the devil did not flag after the Middle Ages. On a number of occasions, Catholic leaders have taken up the topic of the devil, substantially preserving Thomistic doctrine and indicating its foundation in the Bible. During the General Audience of June 3, 1998, John Paul II even spoke of Christ's "characteristic activity as exorcist." In the desert, Jesus began a struggle with the devil that continued throughout his life, in Wojtyla's view. On a number of other occasions, the Polish Pope has spoken of the devil: for instance, in his speech of July 23, 1986, in which, in keeping with Thomistic doctrine, he made a clear theological distinction between good and bad spirits. The good spirits, said the Pope, have chosen God as the supreme good, with all the force of their freedom and love; the others have turned their backs on God, making a radical, irreversible choice.[38] Even for the angels, claims Wojtyla, freedom means the possibility to make a choice for or against the good that they know: that is, God himself.[39] An absolute stability of good, however, can exist for no creature created by God.

Popes have claimed to base their discourses regarding the devil on the Bible. The devil's existence cannot be proven by reason alone; nor can the existence of angels, after all. What we know depends on the revelation known through the Bible. In the Old Testament, for instance, in the prologue to the book of Job, we find the presence of a devil bent on disproving Job's piety. From one minute to the next, one expects the just man to rebel against God. In the New

Testament, one of the most quoted passages is 1 John 3:8:
"This was the purpose of the appearing of the Son of God,
to undo the work of the devil."

We do not have time here to consider the devil in
medieval literature. The devil appears in many works as
early as the 8th and 9th centuries, in the *Lives of Saints* in
the 9th century, and in sermons given by preachers. In
medieval literature, the devil is "used" to tempt saints. He
shows no pity, challenging them indefatigably; but he is
always defeated. The Prince of Evil must now be fought
through exorcism. The early exorcisms were simple in
form. Invocations of Christ and the Virgin Mary, and the
sign of the cross made with true faith were sufficient to condemn the devil to a fiery abyss of stinking sulfur. In Dante's
Divine Comedy, devils are often presented as enemies of
each other. In medieval drama, the devil is presented as a
ridiculous personage, with clownish, vulgar, burlesque
attributes. He often parodies liturgical rites, as in J. B.
Russell's *Il diavolo nel medioevo*.

The Devil in the Italian Renaissance

In this brief study, I do not propose to investigate individual cases of diabolic possession in the Italian Renaissance.
A number of books already exist on that topic.[40] My cen-
tral aim is rather to place in context Girolamo Menghi's
formulas for exorcism, first published in 1576.[41] Menghi's
work represents a high point in the vast demonological literature that the cultural and religious imagination produced during the Renaissance and the period immediately
following—before Pope Paul V, anxious to establish some
order in the unfathomable, archaic world of the devil,
imposed the so-called *Rituale Romanum* in 1614 for those
practicing exorcism.[42]

Indeed, it must be remembered that magic, occultism,
and fascination with the exorcist's rites were as deeply

rooted in the Renaissance mentality and culture as they had been in the medieval mind. During the Renaissance, religious problems were studied with greater critical awareness. Greater attention was given to the human condition, to our inner feelings and thought processes, independent of the Church and its dogma. Attempts were made to harmonize art, religion, and other aspects of culture with a classical ideal of beauty. The Scriptures were certainly not neglected, but scholars claimed some right to autonomous judgment. Pico della Mirandola, writing to his nephew Giovannino, says: "You can do nothing more useful for yourself than to dedicate yourself day and night to the sacred scriptures *(Nihil Deo gratius, nihil tibi utilius facere potes quam si non cessaveris litteras sacras nocturna versare manu, versare diurna.)*"[43] This passage reflects what became known as *docta pietas,* a continued passion for humanistic culture, coupled with a passion for Christ. Men frequently expressed the need for a renewed Church, one more closely identified with the gospel and the spirituality of the early Church. Virtue is the work of the will, observed Salutati in his *De saeculo et religione,* attempting to shake the ecclesiastical hierarchy out of the moral softness into which it had fallen.[44] In an uneasy atmosphere of anticipated renewal, exorcisms may have seemed to represent a step backward; but from the point of view of institutional power, they had the opposite effect. They were a powerful instrument for reinforcing the power of the hierarchy, which, ironically, tried to dominate people through the devil. The devil was presented as the reality of evil, from which only the Church and its rites could liberate us. While humankind increased its dominion over the visible, the Church responded by taking possession of the invisible.

The Renaissance was fraught with conflict and contradiction. Religious certainties that, until then, had supported the spiritual and social assumptions of Christendom were now called into question. The Church of Rome gradually lost its monopoly on truth; the profession of faith often became a dramatic choice on which, in extreme cases, one's life depended. Individuals or groups accused of heresy, witchcraft, or sorcery were mercilessly hunted down. Even after the Council of Trent, the Church led a harsh battle against anyone who expressed doubt about its doctrinal foundations. The Sant'Uffizio had the task of discovering and bringing to trial heretics, "witches," and dissidents. Books considered dangerous for the faith and morality were included in the Index of Forbidden Books and burned or expurgated in successive editions. Michelangelo's *Universal Judgment*, with its nudes, was threatened with destruction (though, in the end, certain nudities were covered). Religiosity became troubled, nervously sensitive, characterized by sentimental abandonment and obsessive scruples. Writers like Torquato Tasso were torn between a desire for freedom and a deep sense of guilt; between perplexities of faith and declarations of orthodoxy. We see a clear example of this in Galileo Galilei's dramatic conflict with the Church as he tried to reconcile Catholicism and the new science. Readings of the Scriptures produced bloody clashes between advocates of different interpretations. Machiavelli had the courage to say that religion had become merely an instrument of social cohesion, with a political function. He blamed the lack of religiosity on the Church: "We Italians thus have this primary debt with the Church and with the priests: to have become without religion, and to have become bad."[45]

When we speak of the civilization of the Renaissance, we must be careful not to mistake the ideal for the reality. The era from the second half of the 15th century to the end of the 16th was a period of violence, conflict, and supreme artistic experiences. In both war and art, one sought support in the Catholic Church.

Many scholars and artists attempted to find favor at the papal court, the richest of its time. Many embraced ecclesiastic careers that offered economic well-being, without demanding much in the way of pastoral care. That explains why many

writers of the early 16th century were ecclesiastics. Bembo
became a cardinal; Castiglione, when widowed, entered the
clergy and exercised diplomatic functions; Menghi wrote
about exorcisms, taking care to dedicate his work to Cardinal
Paleoto in order to obtain his support. The Sant'Uffizio's attention was soon drawn to him, however, and his works were
placed on the Index. They disappeared from circulation, only
a few copies remaining in monastery libraries for the benefit of
monks and a few privileged scholars.

After the exile to Avignon and the occidental schism, the
Church lost political and moral authority. Many popes
behaved like frivolous princes, keeping corrupt courts. This
did not, however, keep them from striking out against those
who dared to criticize them—like Savonarola, with his passionate temperament and colorful language.

It was into this philosophic and religious atmosphere
that Girolamo Menghi was born, in Viadana, Italy, in the
province of Mantua. In his time, he enjoyed fame as a religious figure, a writer, and an exorcist. An erudite
Renaissance scholar, he collected material concerning
demonology and exorcism from codices, manuscripts, and
printed books. He expressed himself skillfully in Italian and
Latin, communicating his passion for the practice of exorcism, his principal mission in life.

After entering the Franciscan order of the Frati
dell'Osservanza in Bologna at the age of twenty, Menghi
studied theology, acquiring fame as a preacher. He became
Superior of a Franciscan province in 1598, with the assistance of Pope Clement VIII. He wrote a number of books on
religious subjects, but those that brought him the most fame
were his works on exorcism. These earned him the title of
"father of the exorcist's art,"and led him to be considered
the greatest exorcist of the 16th century. His three best-
known works in Latin were *Flagellum daemonum* (1576),
Fustis daemonum (1584), and *Remedia probatissima in
malignos spiritus expellendos* (1579). His most famous

work in Italian was *Compendio dell'arte essorcistica* (1576).

Menghi's work can truly be characterized as a fore-runner of modern studies on demonology, although it is still marked by the influences of medieval magic that colored works from a preceding era. He is well acquainted with demoniacal literature: the authors he quotes range from Avicenna to Michael Psellus, from Raymond Lull to Pietro da Palude; from Silvestro Prierio to J. Sprenger, the writer of *Malleus maleficarum*. In the early 18th century, his works were struck down by the Sant'Uffizio and included in the Index of Forbidden Books.

Many of Menghi's works brought him great success as soon as they were published. The most famous ones were *Compendio dell'arte essorcistica*,[46] published in 1576, and *Flagellum daemonum,* a series of exorcisms composed in Latin, which he himself described as *"terribiles, potentissimi et efficaces"* in their action against the devil. Another important book is his *Fustis daemonum* (*Club Against Demons*), which appeared in 1584.[47] Throughout his career, this erudite, pious friar was vitally caught up in his studies of demons and exorcism. He defines the doctrine to which he dedicates himself *"pulcherrima et valde necessaria"* ("most beautiful and extremely important").

Menghi believed his mission to be beneficial; he felt a pressing moral obligation—"not having come into the world for myself," he explains, "but also for the good of my neighbor."[48] He compares himself to the ancient fathers and doctors of the Church, who worked dynamically in order to uproot heresies and maintain the integrity of Christian doctrine . He repeatedly affirmed the fundamental unity of God the creator: the devil, he insists, was created by God, and created good. He supported his views with the words of the church councils, and of the Scriptures.[49] In chapter 2, we will explore Menghi's view of evil and the role it played in the social and religious life of his era.

GIROLAMO MENGHI'S
VISION OF EVIL

Girolamo Menghi articulated a philosophy of evil that reflected the social and religious culture of his time. He firmly rejected the Manichaean dualistic vision: the devil, he claimed, is evil, but he is not Evil. To avoid any absolute, polar duality between Being which is good and Being which is evil, Menghi imagined a scale ranging from good to evil. He tried to arrange devils according to their functions, spheres of action, and bad habits—just as Pseudo-Dionysius the Areopagite had arranged angels in his *Celestial Hierarchy*.

In order to explain differences in behavior, strength, and natural perfection that devils exhibit in relation to the human sphere, Menghi divided demonic spirits into hierarchies. For example, devils of the lowest order, *l'infimo choro*, acted within the lowest sphere; even when harming people, they did so with less malice. These spirits of *l'infimo choro* often came out at night, raucously playing their little

tricks "*fra burle, giuochi e altre cose da scherno.*"[1] These
are the devils that Italians call elves—*foletti*. Then there are
the *incubi* and *succubi*, demons who specialized in lewd
nightly invitations, urging people on to frivolous sexual
pleasures. These devils, he notes, soil and stain us with the
sin of lust.[2]

Menghi gives a colorful description of demonic orders
or groups, based on the authority of Michael Psellus, a
Byzantine philosopher (1018–1078). A counselor at the
court of Constantinople, Psellus had written a booklet entitled *De daemonum energia, seu operatione*, in which he
portrayed demons as physical beings capable of influencing
bodies. He described their bodies as dark and obscure, contrary to angelic bodies that were usually described as
devoid of matter and perennially luminous. Moreover, he
held that demons loved entering the bodies of animals and,
better yet, humans, in order to receive some heat.

Menghi called the first group of demons the *Leliureon*,
or "fiery ones."[3] This group was constituted of demons
who wandered high in the air, "near fire," perhaps meaning
near the Sun. The name itself is sonorous, rhythmic, luminous; it is hard to imagine it attached to beings that try to
push us into the abyss of eternal evil and pain.

The second order of demons, the *Aerea*, is made up of
demons present in the air nearest us. These demons are
proud and haughty, and drive us to vainglory and conceit.
They bear within themselves a persistent, sad fascination
with measuring themselves against God, thus going against
nature and their own reality. Of course, their aspirations
are destined to miserable failure.

The third order of demons is called the *Terreo*, since
they abide on Earth and base their temptations in Earthly
matters. After all, it is petty, Earthly interests that most
often drive even the best of us to lose moral control. The
Terreo are followed, in Menghi's hierarchy, by the
Acquatile or *Marino*, who operate mostly in humid, watery

places—seas, lakes, and rivers. They cause storms at sea, sinking ships that are full of people and goods: *"cariche di huomini e pretiosissime merci."*[4] It is hard for us to imagine such diabolical deep-sea divers immersed in the watery depths, drifting over the sea floor, set on the arduous task of sinking boats large and small. It is somehow easier to think of devils among crowds, in shops, at the market, in bars, among faces exuding oil and sweat.

Next come the *Sotterranei*, who torment those who work beneath the surface of the Earth and cause earthquakes that shake the foundations of buildings.[5] They destabilize things, and may even throw stones. These are truly cruel devils, who enjoy hurting those who have a hard enough time getting by as they toil in mines, far from the light, risking death at every moment. Menghi says, however, that such devils are easy to identify and conquer; even a little old woman, he claims, could easily drive them off. Beware, however, he warns: the *Sotteranei* often become the docile servants of magicians and sorcerers.

The sixth and last group is the *Lucifogo*, so called because they flee from the light, and are dark and mysterious. You had better stay away from them, since they can coldly kill you: *"possono con freddezza violentemente ammazzare gli huomini."*[6] The *Acquatile*, *Sotterraneo*, and *Lucifogo* are the worst, Menghi concludes, although the *Aerei* and *Terreni* do arouse filthy, iniquitous thoughts.[7]

Demons, Menghi claims, are not only crafty, but learned as well. They know the truth of things in three ways: by experience, by revelation, and by nature.[8] From experience, they know the inclinations of people, and so can foresee the evil they have done and may do. They bet on the possibility of predicting human reactions in given situations. Through revelation, they know that, in creating them as superior spirits, God granted them the possibility of knowing themselves and others. By nature superior, they know inferior nature, and so can somehow dominate it.

God gave them perfect intellect, memory, and will, so that they are able to know human reality and foresee future actions.

Menghi says that the devil "sees everything contained in known reality," "all kinds of things created by God, whether physical or spiritual."[9] The devil knows our illusions, deceits, moral shortcomings, disappointments, interests, and abuses. Menghi believes the devil to be an acute philosopher, mathematician, grammarian, and theologian, capable of knowing future events that depend on the capacity of their own intelligence and experience. The devil knows the evil that will be done, and the means and ways in which it will be actuated. From this knowledge, he draws probable conclusions. However, as regards the intimate secrets of the human heart, he knows only what God allows him to know, for the ends that God himself chooses. What humans experience and suffer is often unexplainable. An exact knowledge of the future based on knowledge of the past is, therefore, not always possible.

In one of his sermons, Savonarola confronts the problem of the angels' knowledge of the future. He notes that God has reserved for himself alone this cognition of what may and may not occur in the future. Angels know those future events that occur through necessary cause, in the same way that we know that an olive tree will produce olives, and wheat will produce wheat.[10]

Demons can move from place to place (Matt. 4) and can possess human bodies in a way that Menghi defines as "virtual quantity."[11] He gives an example through comparison: The devil acts within the body of the possessed just as the word of one who speaks arouses joy or suffering in the heart and mind of the listener, or as the Moon, with its potency, its *virtù*, touches the mind of lunatics till they go mad.[12] Menghi defines as "virtual" that immaterial reality that enters into contact with material reality. Demons, he adds, also have the capacity to appear in human form (as did Christ). They are not subject to bodies, but dominate them, since spiritual nature is higher than physical nature.[13] The superior reality of the spirit rules over matter. The quality of the spiritual entity is not presented by Menghi in opposition to matter, but rather as energy dominating it. Matter loses all strength, becoming manipulated and actualized by spirit.

Demons may even take on the appearance of a saint, or of Christ himself. Menghi points out that, in the *Lives of the Holy Fathers*, we find a hermit to whom the devil appeared in the form of a beautiful woman, who seduced him to the "filthy act of lust"; but just as he was aroused to perform the act, she ran off, ridiculing him.[14] One must always beware of the devil. Even the strongest will can fall to instinct, to passion. Spiritual pride is thus humbled. Strength and weakness, light and damnation, are in constant tension in us. Unexpected fractures, even abysses, can suddenly appear in the conscience.

When the devil takes possession of human bodies, he can even put on a show of magic tricks, making his victim vomit nails, knives, or stones. Are these medieval tales that our exorcist accepts as true? He speaks of a girl in Bologna who, before his very eyes, vomited similar objects. Can we believe him? He seems to speak in good faith. He himself does not consider the possibility of self-illusion resulting from his immersion in the demoniac-spiritual dimension.

Indeed, Menghi often seems to accept the impressions of authors who preceded him without adopting any degree of critical awareness. He affirms that witches and magicians "make men impotent, so they cannot use matrimony with their own wife; or the woman cannot conceive."[15] Witches, he says, can obscure the minds of all people except judges, because "all those who exercise public justice are ministers of God."[16] Moreover, demons can eat and drink, according to Menghi, even though they do not digest food, which is dissolved back into its pre-existing matter—"*nella preiacente materia*"—as occurred in the case of Christ, who ate after the resurrection, with his glorious body.[17]

Since the powers of the devil are so extraordinary that he can assume the form of men or women, Menghi concludes that they can also have sexual relations and generate children.[18] Some people have witnessed witches lying with the devil. Some even speak of men who have seen their women lying with the devil; at the moment when, in their rage, they took up arms to wound and kill the couple, the devil immediately disappeared.[19] Menghi tells of a young nun who revealed to her spiritual father that "the devil often had carnal relations with her against her will"; she showed repentance over that fact.[20] Menghi's wholehearted enthusiasm in relating such scabrous episodes is untempered by the expression of any doubts.

The foregoing discussion might lead some to think that Menghi thought we are not responsible for any of the evil we do, that our sins can be blamed almost wholly on the multiform, potent instigations of the devil. In fact, however, Menghi takes care to tell us that our will always remains dominant. Helped by grace, it can serenely oppose evil.[21] Is it possible, asks Menghi, that the devil's tricks can dull and deceive the senses, and weaken our powers of will and intellect, inexorably making us give in to his bold suggestions? No, he concludes. The mind remains awake and functioning; otherwise, sin would not exist. In order to rehabilitate free will, Menghi is forced to attenuate the implacable action of the devil and revitalize our power of choice. The devil actuates only what Menghi calls "hidden persuasion." For example, the devil can make a man encounter a woman in a given place if he perceives that a disorderly love can arise from the encounter. He can even alter the mind a bit, as wine does, "*sì come si vede negli ubbriachi*."[22] But the devil cannot make man commit sinful, lustful acts. The devil, he emphasizes, never tires of acting.

Menghi describes certain witches, or *lamie*, who play tricks of all sorts. The lamie have sexual relations with devils as *incubi* or *succubi*, renounce their faith and the sacraments, and adopt the holy cross to adore the devil.[23] Some *lamie* make pacts with the devil, who promises them to "make all things happen that will be prosperous to their will."[24] The devil makes precise demands, however. For example, the person must spit on the ground when the most holy body of Christ is elevated, during the Eucharist; or one must never confess one's mortal sins, and must deny and despise the Christian faith.[25] There are secret, solemn rituals used, according to Menghi, to become part of the devil's army. Candidates are led before the devil, who commands them to renounce the faith, baptism, and all the sacraments. They are also obliged to show scorn for the images of Christ, Mary, and the Saints. They must swear fidelity to the devil in body and soul, again promising to find him proselytes: girls and boys willing to give up their faith. The disciple must swear full subjection to the devil, just as the faithful swear adherence to any religion. The promise essentially consists of an oath never to return to the worship of Christ. Candidates must then dedicate a nocturnal sacrifice to the devil, adoring him as if he were God. During the ceremony, initiates are assigned a demon, called "Martinetto," who will train them and accompany them always. During the nightly rites, initiates participate in lustful pleasures of the flesh.[26]

The Martinetto, disguised as a ram, accompanies the candidates to the nocturnal ceremonies. Everyone dances, abandoning themselves to "amorous carnal pleasures."[27] "Each demon takes up the woman to whose custody and rule he has been assigned, and with her he dances and makes merry."[28] Everyone eats and drinks; the lights go out, and men and women join together. They promise never to make the sign of the cross, and to draw as many people away from God as they can. Menghi also speaks of the cruel rites that occur during these diabolic encounters: "They eat the children of their own species, and those they do no eat remain in the devil's power; they offer them to the devil, or kill them, especially when they are unbaptized, so that, not having taken baptism, they cannot rise to the glory of paradise."[29]

Endowed with demonic power, these initiates can manifest occult things, or predict the future "for the devil's information," arousing wonder and winning over new followers. They often know how to cause abortions and kill babies in the mother's womb. They can bring harm with a single glance, so, Menghi warns, you must stay away from them.[30]

The conflict between God and the devil, between the light and darkness, is ancient. In Menghi's time, this conflict was exacerbated by exorcists and their audiences, dramatized till it became a tragic, horrifying, grotesque event. The monstrous, violent elements, sinister and fascinating, are exalted in Menghi's writings, creating in the reader a sublime yet aberrant atmosphere, along the lines of a mythico-religious model.

Delirium, desecration of the "holiest" things, wild experiences fanned by uncontrolled passion, states that are part of our modern obsessed, troubled consciousness, are here seen as proof of the will to follow the devil. Other logical conclusions follow: If God is Sun and light, night belongs to the devil, being more propitious to the most uncontrolled forms of action involving love and death.

Menghi informs us that those possessed by devils are called "stinkers"—*fetoni*.[31] He agrees with those who advocate the strict application of existing laws against magicians and witches, given the great evil caused by them. If magicians are well known, they must be denied communion; if they wish to change their lives, they must be punished and made to subsist for forty days on bread and water in order to purify themselves.

Menghi warns us that even individuals of great piety

and moral integrity may be invaded by unclean spirits.[32] Being possessed by the devil, he says, is not a sin in itself. Indeed, why this occurs is a mystery. Some speak of personal blame in such cases, some of trials useful for sanctification. In any case, exorcisms should be performed with serenity; it is God who operates by way of ministers who have led exemplary moral lives, and by way of the participants' prayers.[33]

In comparison with other writers who traffic in the more scabrous aspects of demonology, Menghi shows no small degree of discretion. He avoids the long, vulgar descriptions into which other writers fall. Friar Zaccaria Visconti speaks of bodies that are transformed into beastly forms, and recommends exorcisms that make use of unmentionable potions.[34] In his *De remediis*, Valerio Polidori, a Franciscan friar from Padua, speaks of using enemas to drive out the devil.[35] Floriano Canale maintains that the devil enters the body in the form of a mouse, and goes out in the form of a frog.[36] Francesco Maria De Capellis, a Capuchin friar from Bologna, accompanies his exorcisms with magic spells.[37]

In the year 700, Clement XI condemned books on exorcism that contained texts different from the *Rituale Romanorum*, but many people today wonder why the Church did not intervene earlier. It is not easy to determine the true reason. The 16th century was a century of crisis in the Church; the Counter-Reformation found some utility in exorcisms practiced with theatrical liturgical forms. It was useful for the Church to spread the news among the people that the devil flees from the relics of saints, from the exposed Eucharist, and at the priest's commands.

One delicate question always remained, however: When do we know that a person is truly possessed by the devil? In cases of demoniacs, Menghi felt that he was facing two personalities: that of the possessed person and that of the devil ruling within. The demon tended to annul the other part of the double personality—a metaphysical aspect despotically canceling out reality. The demoniac wavered between awareness and unawareness of the phenomenon. He remained stunned, spellbound in the predicament, but longed to be free of the tormenting delirium. Exorcism, as seen by the Church, was a sacrament, effective *ex opere operato*—that is, it acted independent of the virtue of the person administering it.

According to Menghi and other authors of his time, victims of diabolical possession exhibited seven main signs.

1. They, the *rudis,* speak or understand languages previously unknown to them.

2. They reveal things that they would normally not know, or predict the future.

3. They demonstrate a physical force well beyond their normal capacity.

4. Normally good, conscientious people show hatred toward priests, the sacraments, everything sacred, parents, friends, and so on.

5. With no apparent cause, they sink into the darkest melancholy and desperation (many writers particularly insist on this aspect).

6. In a rage, they blaspheme and invoke the devil's assistance.

7. They vomit knives, keys, pieces of glass, or other objects.

A number of authors fervidly complete one anothers' accounts of the devil, arriving at a sort of convergence: devils are supernatural, but they are absolutely involved with human realty. Humans are destined to be put to the test by temptation, by the subtlest, most unfathomable snares of the devil. Menghi paints such ambiguous personages as elements in a pre-established harmony. Wherever the circumstances of life and human experience take us, we cannot flee the implacable tempter. He follows us, aware of our smallest movements. We are beset by an interminable chain of psychological abuses: in the abysses of evil, in the threatening cracks of rocks, in any labyrinth of life, the devil's rope can reach us.

To what degree does this vision reflect a mythical vision of our inner conflicts? How many of the "devil's" temptations come from within our souls? Are we our own devils? While St. Paul often speaks of an autonomous diabolical presence, St. James claims that God tempts no one to evil; we ourselves are seduced by a malignant force that we bear within ourselves, and which generates sin and death (James 1:13–15).

All of us occasionally feel like victims of a presence that pitilessly pursues us. From this conviction, passage to the demonic is brief. Someone is waiting out there to deceive us. Someone who lives on lies and tricks; a nomad, a diasporic being who has nothing to lose. Ruining souls is his vocation. Perhaps he, too, thinks he is being pursued, having lost faith in any salvation.

INTRODUCTION TO THE
PRACTICE OF EXORCISM

In his book, *Flagellum daemonum,* Girolamo Menghi dedicates many pages to instructing practicing exorcists. He carries out this task with the attitude of one revealing secret truths, reserved only for the courageous few.

The author starts out by expressing bitterness over the profound spiritual crisis characterizing his time. In the air, he perceives a certain *aegritudo,* a malignant atmosphere threatening not only physical health, but also that of the soul.[1] Human conduct, he observes, tends toward corruption, and many individuals are sorely vexed by demons and evil spells.[2] Unfortunately, according to Menghi, people continue to live as if this were not happening around them. Menghi complains that there are few religious souls instructed in the ways of exorcism; that he is forced to live in a time when the arts of exorcism are unknown.[3] Exorcism, he points out, is a necessary mission; the exorcist must by moved by pity.[4] The friar laments the fact that there are few books about exorcism in circulation, and that those are obsolete. He does his best to fill that void.

The work of an exorcist is arduous, he notes—"*opera misericordiae et* laboriosissima."[5] It requires a well-tested faith in Christ, and "painful" contrition for one's own sins. Purity of heart is indispensable for the efficacy of the exorcist's prayers, which draw force "*ex parte ecclesiae,*" from the reserve of sanctity in the Church and its representatives.

Exorcists must approach the possessed soul with a sense of their own unworthiness, with profound humility, for they are only *instrumentum Dei*: a means God uses to perform his works. Exorcists must ceaselessly exhort the subject to purify his or her conscience and humbly prepare to collaborate in the desired liberation. Those who practice exorcism, insists Menghi, must be morally sound, prepared to confront the devil's most violent reactions. When they utter his prayers and the holy names of God, Christ, and the saints, the demoniac will obsessively twist about, exploding in expressions of pain or sudden furor. One must remember that the devil hates everything that is sacred; he accuses, challenges, ridicules, in the most macabre, burlesque, outrageous manner. Exorcists must betray no uncertainty or take any half-measures. They must attack the devil with holy water, incense, and herbs such as herb-of-grace. The devil is troubled; he is desperate, but can not communicate his disquietude and his desperation except through the possessed person. A sign of his presence, then, will be to dispose the demoniac's spirit to darkest melancholy.

Menghi believes that listening to sacred music can bring relief to a soul possessed, calming violent gestures and restoring serenity. The devil greatly fears the music of Guido d'Arezzo—*musica guidonensis*—Menghi claims.[6] Of the effect of herbs, however, he seems less certain. At any rate, Menghi ends his discourse by saying that even devils enjoy some things and suffer because of others. For example, they favor dark, solitary, underground places. He defines demons as lovers of darkness, sadness, and melancholy.[7] Exorcists must be careful never to let up in their struggle against demons, but if necessary, must attack them using harsh words and curses.

Since exorcists are facing a true enemy of God, they are allowed to use scornful words.[8] Furthermore, they must take great care in asking the devil questions; they must not do so in a spirit of curiosity, but only in order to better manage a confrontation with the Evil One. They may ask the devil if the monstrous presence in that creature of God is the work of a single devil or of a legion; they may investigate in order to discover why that person has been chosen instead of another; they may inquire as to when and how to put an end to the torment; and they can ask what saint can be invoked in a particular case. They may ask the devil's name, and the name of his commander.

In praying, exorcists must enounce some fundamental truth of faith, such as the belief in God One-in-Three; humbly, they will kneel, and bow, and strike the ground three times with their head, as a sign of adoration for the Holy Trinity.[9]

Menghi notes that exorcists customarily adopt *res sensibiles*, such as relics of saints and crucifixes. They should do this with extreme caution, however. They must bear in mind that devils often pretend at first to fear these sacred objects. If the objects turn out not to be true relics, the devil will ridicule them as futile objects, bringing incalculable spiritual harm to those present, who often lose faith in true relics as a result.[10] The *res sensibiles* that exorcists have always used, says Menghi, include exorcised olive oil, salt, and water.

Exorcisms require a great deal of energy, so that the weak are often exhausted by them. In order to resist, one must possess patience, fortitude, and perseverance. At certain moments, such toil may seem useless, whereas, for devils, exorcisms are like violent strokes of the whip.[11]

The spiritual dimension of the subjects must be nourished. When they have intervals of physical or spiritual
serenity or are lucid and capable of understanding, they
may receive the Eucharist, notes Menghi. This sacrament
may coexist with a period of demonic possession, as long as
there is no danger of vomiting.[12] On this point, however,
not all the experts agree, given the spiritual turbulence
undergone by the conscience during periods of possession.

Everything that the demoniac touches must be exorcised
or blessed: bedding, clothing, food, the entire dwelling.
There may be cases calling for the person to abandon the
dwelling, for the devil contaminates everything with which
he comes in contact. Any evil instrument must be burnt.

In Chapter XI, of *Flagellum daemonum*, Menghi
presents a few general instructions to follow in practicing
exorcisms:

1. Exorcists must have great faith in their mission; they
   must be moved by a desire to glorify God. It is God who
   is operating here.

2. Exorcists must prepare for the prayers of exorcism by
   fasting and abstinence, which refine the spirit and keep
   concupiscence at bay.

3. Exorcisms must be celebrated following the rites and
   customs of the Catholic Church. Menghi incessantly
   exalts the role of the community in the rites.

4. Before taking up the concrete action of exorcism, ministers must be sure they are facing a case of true diabolic
   possession, not one requiring the intervention of doctors, astrologers, or theologians.

5. Exorcists must constantly illustrate and clarify the
   exorcistic activity: a purely spiritual work, highly worthy in the eyes of God. In no way must there be cause
   for scandal or evil (*ruina*) toward those present.

The greatest discretion must be used. If, at a given place or time, it becomes impossible to reconcile the gravity of execution with the external environment, the exorcism must not be celebrated, or else must be celebrated in another time or place. The minister must never adopt objects such as rings or particular stones in the hope of drawing the devil from hiding through superstitious practices—as if the effect depended on the stars. Exorcism has nothing to do with these practices, Menghi assures us. The patient may, instead, be blessed by invoking the power of Jesus Christ.[13] For the rest, one must accept the will of God, and the times chosen by him for the liberation of the possessed person.

In Chapter XII of *Flagellum daemonum*, Menghi, a man of great experience in the field, puts the immature exorcist on guard. One must know well the insidious snares of the devil in order to defend oneself. For example, when you least expect it, the devil may try to hide—*quaerit latere*. He may stop torturing the aflicted soul and seem to disappear forever. The possessed person, however, may continue to perceive his presence. The exorcist must seek out the devil and command him to say where he is hiding. Sometimes, during the exorcism, the devil may suddenly appear, distracting the mind of the demoniac and, by way of moans and shouts, disturb the exorcist—*"incitando adstantes ad nugas"*—involving those present in stupid jokes.[14] At this point, exorcists must be decisive. If necessary, they must address the devil using ridiculous names, such as *Fachinus, Pistor, Cocus Acherontis*: dirty baker, infernal cook.

Occasionally, the devil moves from one point to another within the victim's body: to the heart, under the neck, to other parts, thus surprising the exorcist and making him or her nervous.[15] Sometimes, the evil spirit momentarily leaves the possessed person, only to return later on. During the separation, the freed person must pray intensely and avoid sexual contact, or at least must not be the direct *causa libidinis,* so that he or she can be totally dedicated to confirming the grace received.[16] If the devil announces he has gone away, he must be asked not to leave in the body "nullum ex sociis"—any of his partners—otherwise the situation will remain as before.

One of the devil's most insidious snares is to convince exorcists that they are dealing with a natural illness, having nothing to do with any diabolic presence. The devil may even arouse dreams in the possessed person, with holy visions of saints or the crucifix, in order to create the sensation that the person is free of demonic persecution. Here, exorcists are put to the test. They must not be distracted from their task, but dedicate themselves to their function with greater fervor than ever. Indeed, they must provoke the devil, prod him, deride him, make him believe he is a fool, even by using threats or commands.

Menghi strives to give practical advice on the little problems that may arise in various circumstances during the practice of exorcisms. He is peremptory. If possible, exorcisms must not be performed in private houses, in order not to create scandal in the weak-minded.[17] Exorcisms must be performed in a church or in a consecrated place dedicated to a saint, in order to guarantee greater participation by the faithful. The choice of place depends on the exorcist's prudence and good sense. It is preferable to avoid the presence of certain "sensitive" women, given the particular nature of the rites; among other things, the devil might break out in unexpected vulgarities.

When should one perform exorcisms? "*Non datur tempus determinatum,*" says Menghi—no particular time is required. Morning is best, however, after Mass, on days dedicated to the great liturgical feasts—Christmas, Easter, and feasts of the Holy Virgin and Holy Apostles.

In answering the age-old question of why the just and those free of particularly sinful behavior are vexed by the devil, Menghi quotes St. Thomas: *"hoc magis pertinet ad rationem penae quam culpae"*—sins have less to do with possession than pain. Possession, he observes, is a pain permitted by God. *"Deo permittente"*—God allows it to happen.[18]

Menghi offers one last piece of advice, from a man who has heard so much vain blathering come out of the mouths of the unscrupulous: exorcists must never remain alone with the person to be healed, both to avoid occasion for scandal or malicious suspicion and because they may need physical or spiritual assistance. Since Christ drove out devils before crowds, it is better to perform exorcisms with the door open. Whoever wants to can thus easily witness the rite, or else just as easily go away.

Menghi is careful to give advice, but he does not narrate facts—not even small facts of diabolic chronicles. One has the sensation that he is passing on his advice spontaneously, after having tested it thoroughly. Whatever may be said of his evident, almost sensuous enjoyment in describing the ins and outs of his practice, his urgency reflects a passionate sense of mission.

PART II

Girolamo Menghi

TERRIBLE AND MIGHTY EXORCISMS EFFICACIOUS IN DRIVING OUT EVIL SPIRITS FROM THE BODIES OF THE POSSESSED

with their blessings
and everything useful for their expulsion

FIRST EXORCISM

Whoever you are—you who are about to exorcise, driven not by a frivolous spirit, but only by necessity or love—prepare yourself to take on this difficult task, first of all, by making a sacramental confession and a fast of three days. While humbling yourself in your heart and remembering that you are a sinner, trust in the power of God, and not in your own. Then you shall enter the church together with the person who is afflicted and tormented by the devil. Before the altar of the Most Holy Sacrament of the Body of Christ, if there is one, or at least before the main altar, genuflect. Then, dressed in the paraments suitable to your Order, with attentive devotion, constancy, and intrepid force, trace upon yourself the sign of the cross ✝—on your forehead, on your mouth, and on your breast—saying the following words:

The sign of the cross ✝ be upon my forehead. The words of Christ ✝ be upon my lips. The weapons of Christ ✝ be within my breast. By the sign of the cross ✝ free us, oh God, from our enemies. Power of the Fa✝ther, give me strength. Wisdom of the S✝on, instruct me. Love of the Holy ✝ Spirit, enlighten me. Blessed be the day and the hour when our Lord Jesus Christ was born of the Virgin Mary. In the name of the Fa✝ther, of the S✝on, and of the Holy ✝ Spirit. Amen. May the Virgin Mary bless us together with her holy Son.

Then he makes the sign of the cross on the forehead, mouth, and breast of the possessed person, saying:

Power of the Fa✝ther comfort him. Wisdom of the S✝on, instruct him. Love of the Holy ✝ Spirit, enlighten him. Blessed be the day and the hour when our Lord Jesus Christ was born of the Virgin Mary. In the name of the Fa✝ther, of the S✝on, and of the Holy ✝ Spirit. Amen.

Then he recites the entire Confiteor:

I confess to Almighty God, to the holy Virgin Mary, to Saint Michael Archangel, to Saint John the Baptist, to the holy apostles Peter and Paul, to all the saints and to you, Father, that I have greatly sinned in thought, word, and deed, through my fault, through my fault, through my most grievous fault. I, therefore, supplicate the holy Virgin Mary, Saint Michael Archangel, Saint John the Baptist, the holy apostles Peter and Paul, all the saints, and you, oh Father, to pray for me to our Lord God.

He absolves the possessed person and those present, saying:

The Lord have mercy on you and, having forgiven your sins, lead you to eternal life. May the almighty and merciful Lord grant you indulgence, absolution, and forgiveness for all your sins.

Then he reads the following commandments:

I command you, demons, who have come to help
the other demons tormenting this creature of God,
[name], on behalf of the Most Holy Trinity, Father,
Son, and Holy Spirit. Subject to the punishment of
being immersed in the pool of fire and sulfur by the
hand of your enemies, subject to the punishment of
surrendering to the hand of your enemies and being
condemned to the pool of fire and sulfur for a thousand years, I command you not to give any help or
favor to the demons tormenting the body of this
creature of God, [name]; instead I order you to
abandon this body and to go straight away to the
places God has destined for you.

Here is the cross †of the Lord: flee, you enemy
forces; the lion of the tribe of Judah has won, the
root of David is victorious.

I also order you, demons who torment this creature of God, [name], to go out from him and to
leave him free and healthy, with no lesion of soul or
body, so that he can serve God, his Creator. And I
also command all your enemies, in the name of the
most holy Trinity, Father, Son, and Holy Spirit, to
force you to obey all my orders and commandments. And subject to the same punishments, I order
you not to say or do anything that might displease
those present or absent, unless you are interrogated
by me. In the name of the Fa†ther, of the S†on, and
of the Holy † Spirit. Amen.

*Then, tying his stole to the neck of the possessed with three
knots, let him say:*

All of you abominable and rebellious spirits, I
exhort and exorcise you, I call and force you, I chal-
lenge and provoke you; wherever you are in this

human being, by means of the Fa✝ther, of the S✝on, and of the Holy ✝ Spirit, by the mighty name of God Elohim, powerful and wondrous, I exorcise and exhort you, I command you with the authority that has been given me, with the power of God and of the most wise Creator, who created everything and keeps you subject to his power from which you cannot flee; I order you, then, to listen to the words of my exorcism and to recognize that you are conquered by the order that has been given you. And now, without my permission, you do not dare to abandon this creature of God and image of God, and thus remain tied and chained, as God's saints tied up the devils with chains, in the same way do I tie you with this stole of jocundity. In the name of the Fa✝ther, of the S✝on, and of the Holy ✝ Spirit. Amen.

Then, laying his hands on the head of the possessed person, he says:

May every power of the devil be extinguished in you, [name], by the imposition of our hands and by the invocation of all the holy angels and archangels, patriarchs and prophets, apostles, martyrs, confessors and virgins, and of all the saints of heaven. Amen.

Then he says the following words, making the sign of the cross on the forehead of the possessed person; and he shall make the sign of the cross each time indicated, unless there is a disposition to the contrary:

Eli ✝, Elohim ✝, Eloah ✝, Eheye ✝, Tetragram[1]✝, Adonai ✝, Shaddai✝, Sabaoth✝, Soter✝, Emmanuele ✝, Alpha ✝ and Omega ✝, First and Last ✝, Beginning and End ✝, Hagios ✝, Ischyròs ✝, ho Theòs ✝, Athànatos ✝, Agla ✝, Jehova ✝,

Homousion †, Yah †, Messiah †, Eserheie †, Christ conquers †, Christ reigns †, Christ rules †. Non-created the Father †, non-created the Son †, non-created the Holy Spirit †. By the sign of the holy cross, free us from our enemies, Oh Lord, our God.

In reading some of the gospel passages below, the priest shall always keep his hands upon the head of the possessed:

Beginning of the Gospel according to John (I:1–14).

In the beginning was the Word:
and the Word was with God
and the Word was God.
He was with God in the beginning.
Through him all things came into being,
Not one thing came into being except through him
What has come into being in him was life,
Life that was the light of men;
And light shines in darkness,
And darkness could not overpower it.
A man came, sent by God.
His name was John.
He came as a witness,
To bear witness to the light,
So that everyone might believe through him.
He was not the light,
He was to bear witness to the light.
The Word was the real light
That gives light to everyone;
He was coming into the world
That had come into being through him,
And the world did not recognize him.
He came to his own
And his own people did not accept him.
But to those who did accept him

He gave power to become children of God,
To those who believed in his name
Who were born not from human stock
Or human desire
Or human will
But from God himself.
The Word became flesh,
He lived among us,
And we saw his glory,
The glory that he has from the Father as only Son of
    the Father,
Full of grace and truth.

PRAISE BE TO YOU, OH CHRIST.

Then may the exorcist add:

By the words of the Gospel, may every diabolical
power be extinguished in you, [name], and may
divine power be infused. Amen.

Then the entire Creed *is recited.*

I believe in God, the Father almighty,
Maker of heaven and Earth;
And in Jesus Christ, his only Son our Lord;
Conceived of the Holy Spirit,
Born of the Virgin Mary,
He suffered under Pontius Pilate,
Was crucified, died, and was buried;
He descended into hell;
The third day he rose from the dead;
He ascended into heaven and sits at the right hand
    of God, the almighty Father;
From there he will come to judge the living and the
    dead.
I believe in the Holy Spirit,
The holy Catholic Church,
The communion of saints,

The remission of sins,
The resurrection of the flesh,
Eternal life. Amen.

And the exorcist says:

Here is the cross ✝ of our Lord Jesus Christ: flee,
you enemy forces, the lion of the tribe of Judah has
won, the root of David is victorious. From the
Gospel according to John (XVI:23–30).

"In all truth I tell you,
Anything you ask from the Father
He will grant in my name.
Until now you have not asked anything in my name.
Ask and you will receive,
And so your joy will be complete.
I have been telling you these things in veiled language.
The hour is coming
When I shall no longer speak to you in veiled language
But tell you about the Father in plain words.
When that day comes
You will ask in my name;
And I do not say that I shall pray to the father for you,
Because the Father himself loves you
For loving me
And believing that I came from God.
I came from the Father and have come into the world
And now I am leaving the world to go to the Father."
His disciples said, "Now you are speaking plainly
and not using veiled language. Now we see that
you know everything and need not wait for
questions to be put into words; because of this,
we believe that you came from God."

Here is the cross ✝ of our Lord Jesus Christ; flee,
enemy forces, the lion of Judah has won, the root of
David is victorious. Hallelujah.

Here the entire Miserere (Psalm 51) *is recited.*

Have mercy on me, O God, in your faithful love,
In your great tenderness wipe away my offences;
Wash me thoroughly from my guilt,
Purify me from my sin.
For I am well aware of my offences,
My sin is constantly in mind.
Against you, you alone, I have sinned,
I have done what you see to be wrong
That you may show your saving justice when you
    pass sentence,
And your victory may appear when you give judgment,
Remember, I was born guilty,
A sinner from the moment of conception.
But you delight in sincerity of heart,
And in secret you teach me wisdom.
Purify me with hyssop till I am clean,
Wash me till I am whiter than snow.
Let me hear the sound of joy and gladness,
And the bones you have crushed will dance.
Turn away your face from my sins,
And wipe away all my guilt.
God, create in me a clean heart,
Renew within me a resolute spirit,
Do not thrust me away from your presence,
Do not take away from me your spirit of holiness.
Give me back the joy of your salvation,
Sustain in me a generous spirit.
I shall teach the wicked your paths,
And sinners will return to you.
Deliver me from bloodshed, God, God of my salvation,
And my tongue will acclaim your saving justice.
Lord, open my lips,
And my mouth will speak out your praise.
Sacrifice gives you no pleasure,

Burnt offering you do not desire.
Sacrifice to God is a broken spirit,
A broken, contrite heart you never scorn.
In your graciousness, do good to Zion,
Rebuild the walls of Jerusalem.
Then you will delight in upright sacrifices—
Burnt offerings and whole oblations—
And young bulls will be offered on your altar.
Glory to the Father, to the Son, and to the Holy Spirit,
As it was in the beginning, is now and ever shall be,
Forever and ever. Amen

Here is the cross ✝ of our Lord Jesus Christ; flee, enemy forces, the lion of Judah has won, the root of David is victorious. Hallelujah.

Psalm 70 *is recited.*

Be pleased, God, to rescue me,
Yahweh, come quickly and help me!
Shame and dismay to those
Who seek my life!
Back with them! Le them be humiliated
Who delight in my misfortunes.
Let them shrink away covered with shame,
Those who say to me, "Aha, aha!"
But joy and happiness in you
To all who seek you.
Let them ceaselessly cry, "God is great,"
Who love your saving power.
Poor and needy as I am,
God, come quickly to me!
Yahweh, my helper, my Saviour,
Do not delay!
    Glory to the Father, etc.

Then it is said:

Do not remember, Lord, our shortcomings, nor
those of our parents, and do not take vengeance for
our sins.

Now the Litanies of the Saints *are recited while kneeling.*

Lord, have mercy.
Christ, have mercy.
Lord, have mercy.
Christ hear our prayer.
Christ answer our prayer.

The following invocations are responded to by saying:

Have pity on him.
Father in heaven, our God
Son, Redeemer of the world, our God
Holy Spirit, our God
Holy Trinity, our God

The following invocations are responded to by saying:

Pray for him.
Holy Mary,
Holy Mother of God,
Holy Virgin of virgins,
Saints Michael, Gabriel, and Raphael,
All of you, holy angels and archangels,
All of you, choirs of saintly spirits,
Saint John the Baptist,
Saint Joseph,
All of you, holy patriarchs and prophets,
Saints Peter and Paul,
Saints Andrew and Thomas,
Saints James and John,
Saints Bartholomew and Matthew,
Saints Matthias and Barnabas,

Saints James and Philip,
Saints Simon and Thaddeus,
Saints Luke and Mark,
All of you, holy apostles and evangelists,
All of you, holy disciples of the Lord,
All of you, holy Innocents,
Saint Stephen,
Saints Lawrence and Vincent,
Saints Fabian and Sebastian,
Saints Ciprianus and Geminianus,
Saints Cosma and Damian,
Saints Gervasius and Protasius,
All of you, holy martyrs,
Saints Sylvester and Gregory,
Saints Ambrose, Augustine, and Jerome,
Saints Martin and Nicholas,
All of you, holy bishops and confessors,
All of you, holy doctors,
Saints Anthony and Benedict,
Saints Bernard, Dominic and Francis,
Saints Ludovicus and Bonaventure,
All of you, holy priests and Levites,
All of you, holy monks and hermits,
Saint Mary Magdalene,
Saints Agatha and Lucy,
Saints Agnes and Cecilia,
Saints Catherine and Anastasia,
All of you, God's saints.

The following invocations are responded to by saying:

Free him, oh Lord.
From every evil and every sin,
From your righteous wrath,
From sudden death,
From the snares of the devil,
From wrath and hate,

From all evil inclinations,
From an impure spirit,
From lightning and storm,
From misfortune and earthquake,
From illness, hunger, and war,
From eternal death;
By your coming and your birth,
By the mystery of your incarnation,
By your baptism and your holy fast,
By your cross and passion,
By your death and burial,
By your holy resurrection,
By your marvelous ascension,
By the coming of the Holy Spirit, paraclete,
On the day of judgment.

The following invocations are responded to by saying:

Hear our prayer.
We sinners.

- So that you will give him peace, hear our prayer!

- So that your pity and mercy shall protect him, hear our prayer!

- So that you will turn toward him the eyes of your mercy, hear our prayer!

- So that, looking upon his tribulation and torment, you will want to relieve him, hear our prayer!

- So that you will bless and free this servant of yours, hear our prayer!

- So that you will want to tear this servant of yours away from diabolical possession, hear our prayer!

- So that this servant of yours will be liberated from diabolical infestations, hear our prayer!

Hear our prayers,
Christ, the Son of God.
Lamb of God, who takes away the sins of the world,
  forgive us, Lord.
Lamb of God, who takes away the sins of the world,
  listen to us, Lord.
Lamb of God, who takes away the sins of the world,
  have mercy on us.

At the end of the litanies these words are repeated:

Here is the cross ✝ of the Lord, etc.

This prayer follows:

PRAYER

Lord Jesus Christ, for the redemption of the world, you let yourself be rejected by the Jews and you were betrayed by Judas with a kiss; you let yourself be tied up with ropes like a meek lamb and you were led to the sacrifice; before Pilate they exposed you, with no respect; you were accused by false witnesses, they pierced your hand with sharp nails, you were covered with the strokes of the whip and offences, with spitting and blows; they crowned you with thorns and raised you on the cross between two criminals; they gave you vinegar to drink and struck you with a spear. Lord Jesus Christ, by these most holy wounds, which I, a miserable sinner, remember, and by your holy cross, I pray that you will not consider my sins nor those of this creature, [name], but according to your great mercy, free him from the torment of the devil. And to me, your unworthy servant, grant the strength to expel all the demons that torment him and to send them to the depths of the abyss by means of your most holy words. You who live and reign forever and ever. Amen.

Here is the cross ✝ of the Lord etc.

Good cross, worthy cross, wood above all other wood. By this sign ✝ of the cross, may every malignant being be rejected, may all evil spirits not wound the mind, and may they flee.

Here is the cross ✝ of the Lord, etc.

Lord, hear my prayer, and may my cry reach you. May your ears bend to hear my prayer. Be for me, Lord, a tower of strength against all evil spirits. Scatter them, Lord, like straw in the blowing wind.

PRAYER

Lord God almighty, origin of every unconquerable power and king of insuperable dominion, who always triumphs in a wondrous way and represses the forces against your reign; who hardily defeats all hostile iniquities and with your word created all things from nothing; who drove from heaven Lucifer and his followers as rebels and proud ones; you who, in your Son, have reconciled heaven and Earth, you do not want the death of the sinner and do not rejoice in the perdition of the dying; you who always forgives and has mercy, have pity on this creature of yours, [name], not considering his sins, but your own benign mercy. Make him free of all bonds with malignant spirits, which keep him chained each day, and from all their disturbances and infestation. As you freed Mary Magdalene from the seven impure spirits and the daughter of the woman from Cana from the torment of the devil, so deign to free this person, [name], from all the evil spirits that haunt him. As you liberated Jonah from the belly of the whale and Susannah from false accusations; and David from the evil sword and from the hands of Saul; and the three children from the burning furnace and Daniel from the lions' den and Isaac from the hands of his father and Joseph from the Pharaoh's prison, so now in your mercy, free this creature of yours,

[name], redeemed by your blood and regenerated in the waters of baptism, and make all torment of evil and diabolical spirits cease for him.

And as you gave your apostles power over the evil spirits and their snares, and made them capable of driving them out of the bodies of men and of curing the sick, now to me, your unworthy servant, regenerated in the waters of baptism and marked with your most holy name, grant through the gift of your grace the strength to drive out these evil spirits from your creature, [name], by means of your power and the invocation of your most holy name. Through Christ our Lord. Amen.

Here is the cross † of the Lord, etc.

PRAYER

God almighty and eternal, Father of our Lord, Jesus Christ, we beg you to command these spirits that hold this servant of yours a slave, [name], to withdraw. Free this servant of yours who believes in the true liberator, our Lord, Jesus Christ, your Son, who lives and reigns with you in the unity of the Holy Spirit, forever and ever. Amen.

Here is the cross † of the Lord, etc.

After the prayers have ended, before beginning the exorcisms against the devils, the priest rises and must exorcise the possessed person in the following manner:

EXORCISM

[Name], I exorcise you in the name of the Father † almighty, of his Son † Jesus Christ our Lord, and with the force of the Holy † Spirit, that you might become a clean body, holy and purified of every stain of iniquity and of all curses, incantations, bonds, evil spells, and sorcery that have been made upon your body and around it.

I, [name], sinner and unworthy servant of God, with the authority that has been given me, in the name of God himself, almighty Father ✝, in the name of Jesus ✝ Christ, his Son our Lord, in the power of the Holy ✝ Spirit, I destroy and want to see destroyed all aforementioned curses, incantations, bonds, evil spells, and sorcery. And I command you, cursed devil, and your companions, to possess no longer the power of remaining in this body, from the soles of the feet to the ends of the hair, but you must immediately go away with all your curses and enchantments. Through Him who will come to judge with fire the living and the dead and the entire world. Amen.

PRAYER

God of mercy, clement God, who, according to the multitude of your mercies, corrects those you love and leads to penitence those whom you accept, we invoke you so that you will deign to grant your grace to your servant [name], who suffers in his body for the weakness of its members. Rejoin to the unity of the body of the Church all that which out of human frailty has been corrupted or violated. Have mercy, oh Lord, on the moaning, have mercy on the tears of one who has no trust except in your mercy, and admit him to the sacrament of your reconciliation. Through Christ our Lord. Amen.

May the possessed person be sprinkled with holy water.

EXORCISM

I exorcise you, [name], who are infirm, but were regenerated with the water of baptism, by the living God ✝, by the true God ✝, by the holy God ✝, by the God who redeemed you with his precious blood, so that you will be free of the devil and so that any ghost and iniquity of diabolical deceit will flee from you, and any impure spirit be driven out. We ask you this through he who will come to judge with fire the living and the dead. Amen.

PRAYER

Oh God, who always rules over your creatures with merciful affection, hear our supplications and look with kindness upon your servant [name], who suffers in his body of a painful malady. Come to visit him and give him the comfort of salvation and heavenly grace. Through Christ, our Lord. Amen.

May the possessed person be sprinkled with holy water. Then with great faith, may the exorcist begin to drive out the demons that are in the body of the possessed person.

EXORCISM

Hear me, filthy diabolical spirit; I warn you and exorcise ☦ you and I command you—vain, senseless, false, heretical, vacuous, inimical, inebriated, foolish, ill-speaking tempter abandoned by the grace of God and Christ. I exorcise ☦ you by means of he who came down to Earth for us, who received his name from the angel, who was made flesh through the working of the Holy Spirit, was born of the Virgin Mary, grew in age, wisdom, and grace; at twelve years of age, he came to the temple and, sitting amid the doctors, interrogated them with wisdom. I command you ☦ through he who was baptized by John the Baptist in the Jordan River, who was tempted by the devil, was sold out and betrayed by his disciple Judas; was taken prisoner, derided, whipped, fed bile, made to drink vinegar, tied and crowned with thorns, stripped of his robes, which were gambled away. I command you ✝ through he who was crucified, died, and was buried, and the third day rose from the dead, ascended into heaven, and sits at the right hand of the Father; from there he will come to judge with fire the living and the dead and the entire world. Immediately come out and flee this body, formed by God, and do not offend either me or those present, nor wound this person in any way. I exorcise you ✝ through that same Christ whose future coming the angel Gabriel announced from the womb of the Virgin Mary and whom John greeted, while still in the womb of Elizabeth; through that same Christ, I order you to respond to me in everything I ask, and to tell me the truth as to the name of your master, your name, whether you are inside or outside this body, whether you are alone or whether you are joined by one or more legions.

Here, the exorcist can ask the name of the devil torment-ing the possessed person, who his companions are, what the name of his master, under what power of demons he is found, why he is oppressing the possessed person, whether the latter is tied up by some spell and how he can be untied, how long he has been in this place, by means of which saint he must come out; then let him ask who are his greatest enemies in heaven, who are his greatest ene-mies in hell, what sign he will give that he is going away. May he also command him not to harm the patient and, in the future, not to dare return or bring bad times. But the exorcist must be prudent and circumspect in his ques-tions, in order not to be deceived. Let him try to liberate the creature of God with the humility of mind necessary for this purpose, rather than speaking with the demons. Once having asked the question, if he has not gone out, whether he has answered or not, let him proceed with the following invocation.

EXORCISM

Reprobate, murderer, son of perdition, I command you ✝ through that same Lord whose sign appeared in heaven; he whom the shepherds went to see and the Magi to adore; he whom the angels and archangels praise together. I order you to come out immediately from this body, creature of Christ; go to the depths of the sea or into the sterile trees or into the wilderness, where there is no Christian habitation or presence of human beings, and there let the sky's lightning burn you. May the sovereign majesty of God, Father, Son, and Holy Spirit, the true Trinity, force you to come out. I exhort you, ✝ iniquitous devil, in the name of Jesus the Nazarene, so that, in hearing the word of the Lord, you will come out of this servant of God. Again, I command ✝ you through he who, when he was born, was greeted by the singing of angels, who said: "Glory to God in the highest." The Magi, come from the East, adored him, offering gold, frankincense, and myrrh, as had been foreseen. I command you ✝ through that same Christ, at whose birth a star appeared in the heavens, as Balaam prophesied: "A star will rise from Jacob" (Num. 24:17). The mute animals recognized him, as was written: "The ox knows its owner and the donkey its master's crib" (Isa. 1:3). I drive you out ✝ through him whom Herod wanted to kill, but could not: in his stead, the holy innocent martyrs were killed, and their blood adorns the holy Jerusalem in heaven. I drive you out ✝ through he who fled to Egypt with his mother, and who at the wedding at Cana changed water into wine; he whom Pilate crowned with a crown of thorns and had crucified; Longinus pierced him with his spear and on the cross he cried: "Eli, Eli, lemà sabactani." I drive you out ✝ in the name of he who was found in the temple among the wise, who was placed on the cross between thieves, suspended in the air; and after the resurrection stood among the disciples, saying: "Peace be with you; it is I, do not fear." I drive you out ✝ through he who died and was buried, went down to hell, drew out his own who were prisoners of the devil and freed the first man, Adam; the third day, he was resurrected and after forty days he ascended into heaven. May he himself drive you out and make you come out of this body and of the members of this creature of God, [name]. May he who drove you from the heavens force you to tell me the name of your master, whether you are alone or have a legion with you. I exorcise you ✝ through he who created the garden of paradise, from which four rivers flow, that is the Gihon, Pison, Tigris, and Euphrates. You wanted to test him, saying, "If you are the Son of God, throw yourself down," and, showing him all the kingdoms of the Earth, you said to him: "I will give you all these, if you fall at my feet and do me homage." I exorcise you ✝ through this same Christ who answered you, saying: "Away with you, Satan! Do not put the Lord your God to the test, for he is the one to whom you must do homage, him alone you must serve."

EXORCISM

Oh iniquitous devil, ancient serpent, I command you ✝ in the name of the most holy God, great and mighty, by the Tetragram that no tongue of the living, nor the mind and understanding of men, can explain. I drive you out ✝ in the name of God, Alpha and Omega; by Jesus, our redemption, life, and resurrection, our defense and salvation, remission of our crimes. I drive you out ✝ in the name of God, Adonai, great and wondrous, ineffable Creator; in the name of the Son of God, inexhaustible Way; in the name of the invisible Spirit, inextinguishable splendor. They are the inseparable Trinity, a lone God invisible, and by all these holy names I command you, devil, to come out immediately from this creature of God, making no offense and without arousing terror in him, without injuring anyone. Leave no sign in him. I command you this ✝ through the Father, the Son, and the Holy Spirit, by the spiritual anointment of God Three in One. Again, I command you ✝ to come out by she who gave Christ her milk and carried her creator in her womb: you no longer have the power to remain in this creature of God, [name]. I order you this ✝ by Saint Michael Archangel, who drove you out of the heavens with the power of God, when he fought against the dragon and defeated it: leave the place where you are now and go into the wilderness or into the depths of the abyss, where you can harm no one. I exhort you ✝ by the holy Archangel Gabriel, who announced to the Virgin Mary the birth and incarnation of our Lord Jesus Christ, when he said: "Hail, Mary, full of grace, the Lord is with you; blessed are you among women." Hearing these words, hurry away from this creature of God, arousing no terror in anyone. I order ✝ you to come out by Saint Raphael, who protected Tobias and Sara and freed them from the devil. With the power of God, he tied up the devil Asmodeus so that he could not harm them in any way. Therefore, I command you to withdraw from this creature of God immediately and never come back, nor start to harm him again. I command ✝ you by all the holy angels and archangels, thrones and dominions, principalities and powers, heavenly hosts, cherubim and seraphim, who everyday without ceasing proclaim in one voice: Holy, holy, holy is the Lord, God of the universe.

EXORCISM

Again, I exorcise you, ✝ accursed devil, by all the prayers of the patriarchs and by the merits of the prophets; by the intercessions of the apostles and the victory of the martyrs; by the faith of the confessors, the prayer of the virgins, and the aid of all the saints of God, who, from the beginning of the world, were pleasing to him. Come out immediately and get away from this creature of God, [name]. Again, I command you, ✝ oh devil, by Abel, who was the first martyr; by Enoch, who walked with God and was taken from the world; by Noah, who was saved from the flood for his uprightness; by the faith of Abraham, who believed in God and received a just reward; by Isaac, who obeyed his father till death, and in this became the figure of our Lord, Jesus Christ, who offered himself for the salvation of the world; by the blessed Jacob, who saw the angel of the Lord come in his succor.

Again, I exhort you, ✝ oh devil, by Moses the holy, with whom God spoke face to face; by the holy prophets Amos, Micah, Hosea, Joel, Obadiah, Habakkuk, Jonah, Zephaniah, Haggai, Zechariah, Malachi, Ezra, Jeremiah, Isaiah, Ezekiel, Daniel, and by all the other holy prophets I order you ✝ to tell me the pure truth in what I am about to ask you and not refuse in any way anything that I shall command from you. Oh devil, I exorcise ✝ you by the prophet Micah, who announced the birth of Jesus in Bethlehem, land of Judah, when he said, "But you (Bethlehem) Ephrathah, the least of the clans of Judah, from you will come for me a future ruler of Israel whose origins go back to the distant past, to the days of old."

I exorcise you ✝ by the prophet Joel, who foresaw the darkening of the Sun and Moon during the passion and death of Christ in announcing: "The Sun will be turned into darkness, and the Moon into blood." Again, I exhort you ✝ by the blessed Jacob, who prophesied the death of Christ, saying: "Let my soul not enter their meeting place, let my heart not join their assembly, for with wrath they have killed men."

I exorcise you ✝ by the holy prophet Zechariah, who announced the temptation of Christ saying: "I saw the high priest Joshua, standing before the angel of Yahweh, with Satan standing on his right to accuse him. The angel of Yahweh said to Satan, "May Yahweh rebuke you, Satan!

May Yahweh rebuke you, since he has made Jerusalem his choice." I exorcise you ✝ by the holy prophet David, who predicted the betrayal of the Messiah by the hand of Judas, his disciple, as narrated in Psalm 41: "Even my trusted friend on whom I relied, who shared my table, takes advantage of me." Again I exorcise you ✝ by the prophet Zechariah, who announced the betrayal of Christ saying: "I took thirty silver shekels and threw them into the treasure of the house of the Lord and they gave them for the vase-maker's field." Again, I exorcise you ✝ by the prophet Isaiah who predicted the coming of Christ saying: "Come, Lord, do not delay, forgive the sins of your people." And again: "the young woman is with child and will give birth to a son whom she will call Immanuel." Again, I exorcise you ✝ by the prophet Habakkuk, who was carried by the angel of the Lord as far as Babylon, above the lions' den where Daniel was. Again, I exorcise you ✝ by the holy prophet Jonas, who for three days stayed alive in the belly of the whale and then stopped to preach in the great city of Nineb. Again, I exorcise you ✝ by the prophet Elijah, who was carried through the sky in a chariot of fire: he prayed that it would not rain on the Earth for three years; then he again prayed that it would rain, and the rain came down and the Earth gave forth its fruits. Again, I exorcise you ✝ by the holy prophet David, whom God chose as king and drew forth from the sheep's pens. I exorcise you ✝ by Daniel, who interpreted the dreams of the king, killed the idol of Baal and was liberated from the lions' den. I exorcise you by the prophet Malachi, who announced the coming of Christ, the judge of the world, saying: "I am coming to put you on trial and I shall be a ready witness against sorcerers, adulterers, perjurers, and against those who oppress the wage-earner, the widow, and the orphan, and who rob the foreigner of his rights and do not respect me, says Yahweh Sabaoth. These do not fear me and you, accursed one, are one of them."

I exorcise you ✝ by the three youths freed from the burning furnace, Sadrach, Mesach, and Abdeneg; and by Saint John the Baptist, of whom none is greater among those born of woman. I exorcise you ✝ by the twelve apostles of our Lord, Jesus Christ, by all his holy disciples and especially by Peter, the prince of the apostles, so that you will immediately come out of this servant of God, [name]; leave his members healthy as you found them when you entered him, and immediately tell me the truth about anything I ask you, without hesitating. Then, by the merits of the saints of God, by my order, with no delay remove yourself entirely from this servant of God, without inflicting any pain, without producing any harm to him, nor to any other person, and, without frightening anyone, go into the depths of the abyss, and do not return from there before the day of judgment. Amen.

Here is the cross ✝ of the Lord, etc.

Here, the exorcist interrogates the devil in order to know whether he has gone out, as said above. Then he proceeds in this way:

I exhort you ✝, ancient serpent, by the judge of the living and the dead, by the creator of the world, by he who has the power to send you to Gehenna, I order you immediately to leave this servant of God, [name], who turns to the fortress of his Church. I exorcise you ✝, not by my weakness, but with the force of the Spirit, and I order you to come out of this servant of God, whom our Lord Jesus Christ made in his image and resemblance. Surrender, surrender, not to me, but to the minister of Christ. May he force you with his power, he who, nailed to the cross ✝, bent you to his dominion. Tremble beneath the arm of he ✝

who tore away from the moaning of hell the souls
of the just and led them to the light. May the
human body arouse terror in you, may the image
of God be terrible to you; do not put up resistance,
do not delay any longer, and get away from this
man, because God has been pleased to inhabit the
human being. And so that you no longer believe
me the weaker and despise me, knowing that I am
a sinner, God himself commands you to do so, ✝
the majesty of Christ commands you, ✝ the Father
commands you ✝, the Son ✝ and the Holy ✝
Spirit command you. The faith of the apostles
Peter and Paul and of all the other apostles commands it of you ✝. The blood of the martyrs commands this of you, ✝ the sacrament of the Cro✝ss
commands it, the divine mystery and power command it. ✝ Jesus the Nazarene commands it of
you, ✝ the Word made flesh commands it. ✝
Come out then, transgressor, come out, oh
tempter full of tricks and deceit, enemy of the
truth. Impious and most obstinate adversary, leave
the space to Christ, in whom you have found none
of your nefarious works; instead, it was he who
stripped you naked, who destroyed your reign,
who conquered you and tied you up, breaking up
your tricks; it was he who cast you into outer
darkness, where ruin is awaiting you and your
acolytes. But why do you stop and think, oh foolhardy one? Why do you go back, oh cruel one?
You are a criminal before God almighty, whose
commandments you have broken. You are a criminal before his son, Jesus Christ, whom you dared
to tempt in such a foolhardy manner, and pre-
sumptuously had crucified. You are a criminal
before the human species, to whom you offered
the fruits of death with your enticements. I exhort

you ✝ then, oh evil dragon, in the name of the immaculate lamb who walked upon the snake and basilisk, who crushed the lion and the dragon, and I order you to leave this man, to leave the church of God. Tremble and flee from the invocation of the name of him whom the infernal depths fear, to whom the heavenly hosts and powers are subject, him whom the cherubim and seraphim praise with ceaseless voices, saying: Holy, holy, holy, Lord God of the universe. Jesus the Nazarene commands you to do this; while you despised his disciples, lying prostrate, he forced you to go out of a man, so that, separating yourself from that man, you did not even foresee that you would end up in a herd of swine. Get away, then, from this man, because I exorcise you ✝ in the very name of the God who formed him. It is hard for you to resist Christ; it is hard for you to rebel against the spur, because, the later you come out, the greater will be the punishment awaiting you. It is not a man whom you despise, but he who is the ruler over the living and the dead, and who will come to judge with fire all men and the present world. Amen.

EXORCISM

Again, I drive you out ✝, oh devil, by means of he who gave his disciples the power to make the blind see, to heal the leprous, to resurrect the dead and cure all infirmities. I exorcise you ✝ by he who redeemed the first man with the wood of his holy cross, who opened the eyes of one born blind, who drew forth from the tomb Lazarus, dead for four days; who with his power cured every illness and destroyed every instrument of magic. By means of this exorcism and of all others, by means of these holy words and prayers, which are celebrated all over the world, I command you, wherever you are or have been, to vanish like smoke and to go into the wilderness or into the depths of the abyss, so as not to harm anyone any longer, nor ever return again.

In the name of the Fa✝ther, of the S✝on, and of the Holy ✝ Spirit. Amen.

SECOND EXORCISM
AGAINST DEVILS ATTACKING
THE HUMAN BODY

In the name of the Fa✝ther, of the S✝on, and of the Holy ✝ Spirit. Amen.

The exorcist shows the demoniac the cross and says:

Here is the cross ✝ of our Lord Jesus Christ; flee, enemy forces, for Christ pursues you. Non-created the Father, ✝ non-created the Son, ✝ non-created the Holy Spirit, the lion of the tribe of Judah has won, the root of David is victorious.

Hail, oh holy cross, by which so many gifts are brought us.

Make me desire what you want and send away everything that harms us. Give me strength, forgiveness, peace, and salvation. You who are my hope in life, be my protection in death. Here is the cross of our Lord, Jesus Christ; flee, enemy forces, for Christ pursues you.

By this sign of the cross, may God send away

every evil being: may they not injure the mind, and may every ghost disappear.

Oh good cross, worthy cross, wood exceeding every other wood. Cross, way of virtue, way of true salvation. Cross, strength of men, that leads us toward the Lord.

Here the exorcist kneels and says:

Almighty God, creator of heaven and Earth; Jesus Christ, king of kings, most high power, you who rule over everything justly and with holy measure, in coming from the heavens you were born of a holy virgin and over the Earth the hand of almighty God extends. After you performed holy miracles in a thousand ways, nailed to the cross, you saved the world with your blood, giving your faithful the trophy of victory with which they can defeat the tricks of the devil. I pray to you, then, oh Christ who loves mankind, to reveal the nefarious works of this devil and, with his very words, demonstrate his evil actions, bringing out the dark poisons. May the people see, and may they praise you forever and ever, may they exalt you in the heavens and on Earth as their creator, you who live and reign with the Father and the Holy Spirit. Amen.

Here, the exorcist rises and, rebuking the devil, says:

Evil devil, great seducer of souls, you who with these evils promise wondrous things, this will be the end for you; they will no longer call you lord, but you will be defeated and derided everywhere you are.

EXORCISM

I exorcise you, oh devil, by the living God and with the force of the Holy Spirit, by he who created you and made you fall from the heavens, by the tremendous day of judgment and by the ineffable name of the Lord: tell me who you are and what your name is.

By these holy names of God, on my command, immediately depart from this creature of God, [name], without inflicting any pain or harming him in any way; immediately come out without wounding anyone. El, ☦ Elohim, ☦ Adonai, ☦ Shaddai, ☦ Soter, ☦ Immanuel, ☦ holy Tetragram (YHWH), ☦ Alpha, ☦ Omega, ☦ Beginning and End, ☦ Hagios, ☦ Ischyròs, ☦ ho Theòs, ☦ Athànatos, ☦ Agla, ☦ Iehova, ☦ Homousion, ☦ Yah, ☦ Jesus ☦ Christ, ☦ Messiah, ☦ Eloah, ☦ Eheye. ☦ Again I exorcise you, ☦ oh devil, ☦ by the living God, ☦ by the true God, ☦ by the holy God, ☦ by means of the Fa☦ther, of the S☦on, and of the Holy ☦ Spirit; by the blessed Virgin Mary, by all the saints of heaven and by everything by which you can be forced and obliged; I command you, oh evil spirit, to show yourself immediately and to answer all my questions.

Here, the exorcist can interrogate the devil who is found in the body, forcing him to tell the truth in everything referring to the liberation of the possessed person. Then the following gospel passages shall be read.

Beginning of the Gospel according to John (1:1–14):

"In the beginning was the Word. . ."

From the Gospel according to Mark (16:14–20):

Lastly, he showed himself to the Eleven themselves while they were at table. He reproached them for their incredulity and obstinacy, because they had refused to believe those who had seen him after he had risen. And he said to them, "Go out to the whole world; proclaim the gospel to all creation. Whoever believes and is baptized will be saved; whoever does not believe will be condemned. These are the signs that will be associated with believers: in my name, they will cast out devils; they will have the gift of tongues; they will pick up snakes in their hands and be unharmed should they drink deadly poison; they will lay their hands on the sick, who will recover."

And so the Lord Jesus, after he had spoken to them, was taken up into heaven; there, at the right hand of God, he took his place, while they, going out, preached everywhere, the Lord working with them and confirming the word by the signs that accompanied it.

PRAISE TO YOU, OH CHRIST.

From the Gospel according to Luke (11:14–28):

He was driving out a devil and it was dumb; and it happened that when the devil had gone out, the dumb man spoke, and the people were amazed. But some of them said, "It is through Beelzebul, the prince of devils, that he drives devils out." Others asked him, as a test, for a sign from heaven; but, knowing what they were thinking, he said to them, "Any kingdom which is divided against itself is heading for ruin, and house collapses against house. So, too, with Satan: if he is divided against himself, how can his kingdom last? You claim that it is through Beelzebul that I drive devils out. Now, if it is through Beelzebul that I drive devils out, through whom do your own sons drive them out? They shall be your judges, then. But if it is through the finger of God that I drive devils out, then the kingdom of God has indeed caught you unawares. So long as a strong man fully armed guards his own home, his goods are undisturbed; but when someone stronger than himself attacks and defeats him, the stronger man takes away all the weapons he relied on and shares out his spoil. Anyone who is not with me is against me; and anyone who does not gather in with me throws away.

When an unclean spirit goes out of someone, it wanders through waterless country looking for a place to rest and, not finding one, it says, 'I will go back to the home I came from.' But on arrival, finding the home swept and tidied, it then goes off and brings seven other spirits more wicked than itself, and they go in and set up house there, and so that person ends up worse off than before."

It happened that, as he was speaking, a woman in the crowd raised her voice and said, "Blessed the womb that bore you and the breasts that fed you!" But he replied, "More blessed still are those who hear the word of God and keep it!"

PRAISE TO YOU, OH CHRIST.

From the Gospel according to Matthew (4:1–11):

Then Jesus was led by the Spirit out into the desert to be put to the test by the devil. He fasted for forty days and forty nights, after which he was hungry, and the tester came and said to him, "If you are Son of God, tell these stones to turn into loaves." But he replied, "Scripture says: Human beings live not on bread alone but on every word that comes from the mouth of God." The devil then took him to the holy city and set him on the parapet of the Temple. "If you are Son of God," he said, "throw yourself down; for scripture says: He has given his angels orders about you, and they will carry you in their arms in case you trip over a stone." Jesus said to him, "Scripture also says: Do not put the Lord your God to the test."

Next, taking him to a very high mountain, the

devil showed him all the kingdoms of the world and their splendor. And he said to him, "I will give you all these, if you fall at my feet and do me homage." Then Jesus replied, "Away with you, Satan! For scripture says: The Lord your God is the one to whom you must do homage, him alone you must serve."

Then the devil left him, and suddenly angels appeared and looked after him.

PRAISE TO YOU, OH CHRIST.

From the Gospel according to Luke (13:6–17):

He told this parable: A man had a fig tree planted in his vineyard, and he came looking for fruit on it but found none. He said to his vine dresser, "For three years now, I have been coming to look for fruit on this fig tree and finding none. Cut it down: why should it be taking up the ground?" "Sir," the man replied, "leave it one more year and give me time to dig round it and fertilize it: it may bear fruit next year; if not, then you can cut it down."

One Sabbath day, he was teaching in one of the synagogues, and there before him was a woman who, for eighteen years, had been possessed by a spirit that crippled her; she was bent double and quite unable to stand upright. When Jesus saw her, he called her over and said, "Woman, you are freed from your disability," and he laid his hands on her. And at once she straightened up, and she glorified God.

But the president of the synagogue was indignant because Jesus had healed on the Sabbath, and he addressed all those present saying, "There are six days when work is to be done. Come and be healed on one of those days and not on the Sabbath." But the Lord answered him and said, "Hypocrites! Is there one of you who does not untie his ox or his donkey from the manger on the Sabbath and take it out for watering? And this woman, a daughter of Abraham whom Satan has held bound these eighteen years—was it not right to untie this bond on the Sabbath day?" When he said this, all his adversaries were covered with confusion, and all the people were overjoyed at all the wonders he worked.

PRAISE TO YOU, OH CHRIST.

From the Gospel according to Mark (9:17–29):

A man answered him from the crowd, "Master, I have brought my son to you; there is a spirit of dumbness in him, and when it takes hold of him it throws him to the ground, and he foams at the mouth and grinds his teeth and goes rigid. And I asked your disciples to drive it out and they were unable to." In reply, he said to them, "Faithless generation, how much longer must I be among you? How much longer must I put up with you? Bring him to me." They brought the boy to him and, at once, the spirit of dumbness threw the boy into convulsions, and he fell to the ground and lay writhing there, foaming at the mouth. Jesus asked the father, "How long has this been happening to him?" "From childhood," he said, "and it has often thrown him into fire and into water, in order to destroy him. But if you can do anything, have pity on us and help us." "If you can?" retorted Jesus. "Everything is possible for one who has faith." At once, the father of the boy cried out, "I have faith. Help my lack of faith!" And when Jesus saw that a crowd was gathering, he rebuked the unclean spirit. "Deaf and dumb spirit," he said, "I command you:

come out of him and never enter him again." Then it threw the boy into violent convulsions and came out shouting, and the boy lay there so like a corpse that most of them said, "He is dead." But Jesus took him by the hand and helped him up, and he was able to stand. When he had gone indoors, his disciples asked him when they were by themselves, "Why were we unable to drive it out?" He answered, "This is the kind that can be driven out only by prayer and fasting."

PRAISE TO YOU, OH CHRIST.

EXORCISM

I exorcise you, ✝ unclean spirit, tempter, devil, lascivious enemy, inebriated and foolish, abandoned by the grace of God and Christ. I exorcise you and I command you by he who came down to Earth for us, was made flesh by the workings of the Holy Spirit, and was born of the Virgin Mary. Come out immediately and, with no delay, flee this body created by God, and do no harm to this or any other person.

I exorcise ✝ you by him whose coming the angel Gabriel announced when he was in the womb of Mary; I exorcise you ✝ by him whom John the Baptist greeted in the womb of Mary before he was born of Elizabeth. By his means, I exorcise you, I exhort and command you, if you are in this body, to speak to me and tell me the name of your master. Oh son of perdition, fraudulent murderer, I exorcise you by him whose sign appeared in the heavens; the shepherds saw him and the Magi adored him; the angels and the archangels together praise him. May he himself drive you out of this body made in the image of Christ and may he send you into the depths of the seas or into the wilderness, where no human habitation lies, and from the sky, may the holy Trinity, Father, Son, and Holy Spirit, burn you. I exorcise you ✝ in the name of Jesus Nazarene, whom King Herod wanted to kill and could not: in his place the holy innocent martyrs were killed, whose blood adorns the heavenly Jerusalem. I exorcise you ✝ and I command you ✝ by means of he who fled into Egypt with his mother.

I exorcise you by the crown of Christ and I exorcise you ✝ by he who, at Cana, turned water into wine, who was crucified under Pontius Pilate, who was pierced by Longinus with a spear as he cried out on the cross: "*Eli, Eli, lemà sabactani.*" He is the same one who went down to hell and drew forth those who were prisoners of the devil; the third day, he arose from the dead and, after forty days, he ascended into heaven. It was he who freed the first man, Adam: may he then drive you out, heretic, false one, murderer, accursed, Christless, and crossless. I exorcise you ✝ and I exhort you by means of he who, from Earthy paradise, made four great rivers spring—Pison, Gihon, Tigris and Euphrates—so that you will have no authority or power to hide your name. And now immediately, tell me who you are and who is your master, for I am the servant and minister of Christ.

Here, may the exorcist ask the name of the devil and of his companions, ask why they are tormenting the possessed person and what remedies are necessary for his liberation.

EXORCISM

Listen, evil devil, accursed creature, reprobate and damned by God, hear how great is your arrogance. You have abandoned God who generated you, you have forgotten your Creator and, for your arrogance, you are condemned to eternal fire together with Satan, prince of demons. I trust in the power and strength of God, creator of the universe, while you, accursed devil and unclean Satan, highly arrogant spirit, you have perverted your election, and with scorn you have abandoned your heavenly domicile, choosing to contradict the orders of God, and refusing to convert to him, our God and almighty Lord, Three-in-One before time began, who is the cause by which all creatures exist, so that, in the blinking of an eye, the world could not continue if it withdrew from his dominion. You, then, did not want to obey God, as did, instead, the highly blessed spirits who enjoy his full happiness, but you were pleased with the perverse order of pride and envy. You chose your fate and that of the angels blinded by your unclean choice, and so you have fallen from the highest heavens and have fallen into this darkness: now, on the tremendous day of judgment, the abyss and pit of hell awaits you, where you will be tormented day and night and the smoke of your torments will rise forever.

I exorcise and condemn you, † whether you are alone or more than one devil, and I order you to tell me how you dared to enter this servant of God, [name], consecrated and initiated in the sacred mysteries; tell me if it was in food or drink or by means of some evil superstition or magic spell performed in any way upon this servant of God. All these spells and curses, and each one in particular, I do dissolve and declare melted in virtue and by the power of Jesus Christ, unconquered king and our savior, who appeared in this world to dissolve the works of Satan. And, like the Lord, by means of the holy apostles Peter and Paul, our fathers, he dissolved the spells and curses of your follower Simon the magician; as through the apostle Bartholomew he healed persons tormented by the devil of Astaroth; and as by means of Moses he unveiled the tricks of the Egyptian sorcerers; so by the power of the same finger of God, that is the Holy Spirit proceeding from the Father and the Son, we dissolve all these spells and curses performed upon this servant of the Lord, [name], whether their cause come from the cruelty of envy with which you, unclean, evil spirit, lay snares to entrap the salvation of men according to your impious desire; or whether this happens by the just disposition of God almighty or because of his sins, or those of his parents. Before all of this, I interpose the copious redemption obtained with the most precious blood of Jesus Christ our Lord, who, out of love for us, washed away our sins with his blood.

In coming into this world, Christ conquered your master, not only with power, but with the price of his blood, and chained him, breaking up his works and stripping him of any power: thus by a strong hand, we have been justly liberated from your dominion. And the same blessed God and Lord, rising into heaven as our master, gave to his disciples and faithful the power to drive you out of the bodies of men, saying: "In my name they will drive out devils." And again, he declared to the twelve apostles: "I have given you power over all the demons and the works of the enemy."

We too, though unworthy, he wanted as participants in this power. In fact, by means of our ministry, he transforms the substance of bread and wine into his body and blood. Now, by virtue of the power that has been granted me by God almighty, and by our Lord, Jesus Christ, I order you to appear, oh unclean spirit, whether you are alone or are several devils, however you dared to enter this servant of God, [name], consecrated and initiated in the divine mysteries, in food, in drink or by means of any evil superstition or spell cast upon him. And I command you in the name of the Father, of the Son, and of the Holy Spirit, to come out and go away from this servant of God, doing harm in no way, and, in the future, dare no longer to approach him or reside within him; do not perturb his inner or external senses, from the soles of his feet to the ends of his hair; do not dry up his bones or move his humors, do not torment him with any malady and do not impede his rest in the hours of night or in the hours of the day.

If you insist on not obeying and on despising our orders and commands, or rather those of God and our Lord Jesus Christ, by the merits of his passion, by the intercession of his mother, the Virgin Mary, and of all the holy angels who see the face of the Father almighty, by the merits of the patriarchs, of the prophets, of the apostles, of the martyrs, of the confessors and of all the holy virgins, we beg him humbly so that, as he did with the hard-hearted, arrogant Pharaoh, he will send against you his holy angels, who will tie you up with chains of fire and sink you together with the other apostate angels who are your allies into the pool of fire and sulfur, where you will be tormented night and day, and the smoke of your torments will rise forever. Amen.

EXORCISM

Accursed devil, damned and reprobate creature, condemned eternally by God for your malignity, unclean spirit, wherever you are hiding in the body of [name], recognize the verdict of just condemnation that has been pronounced upon your iniquity. Though forced and obliged against your evil will, render honor to the true and living God, ✝ render honor to Jesus Christ, his Son, our Lord and Savior, ✝ render honor to the Holy Spirit paraclete ✝ and get away from this servant of God, [name], and no longer approach him, for the Lord Jesus has deigned to call him to his holy grace and blessing with the gift of baptism. And never dare to violate this sign of the holy ✝ cross, which we put upon your forehead, you, accursed devil, damned and damning, unclean spirit, in the name and by the power of the same Lord of ours, Jesus Christ, who will come to judge with fire the living and the dead and the entire universe. Amen.

Here, the exorcist lays his hands upon the head of the possessed person and says this prayer.

Expel, oh Lord, the devil from this creature of yours, [name], from his head, from the ends of his hair, from his forehead, from his eyes, from his tongue, from underneath the tongue, from his ears, from his nostrils, from his neck, from his jaws, from his teeth, from his throat, from his gums, from his mouth, from his palate, from his brain, from the folds of his brain, from his eyelashes, from his eyebrows, from his hairs, from his feet, from his tibias, from his knees, from his legs, from his shameful parts, from his back, from his sides, from the upper and lower intestines, from his thighbone, from his belly, from his stomach, from his heart, from his shoulder blades, from his shoulders, from his chest, from his breasts, from his arms, from his hands, from his fingernails, from his bones, from his nerves, from his veins, from his bone marrow, from his lungs, from the structure of his body, from all the joints, from all his body, inside and outside, from the five senses of the body and soul. May the devil find no more place in this creature, either inside or outside, so that he will be safe and sane by invocation of the most holy name of your only-begotten Son and by invocation of the Holy Spirit, co-eternal with you. You, then, almighty God, who deigned to create the body and soul of this creature, [name], also deign to save and redeem his entire body and his entire soul. By the same Christ, our Lord. Amen.

Third Exorcism
EXCELLENT AND OF WONDROUS EFFICACY AGAINST THE EVIL SPIRITS

Kneeling, the exorcist, with a firm, devout spirit, says:

Our help is in the name of the Lord

HE MADE HEAVEN AND EARTH.

Blessed be the name of the Lord

NOW AND FOREVER.

Kyrie eleison, Christe eleison, Kyrie eleison.
Our father. . . *(all recite the Lord's Prayer)*

PROTECT, OH LORD, THIS SERVANT OF YOURS WHO HOPES IN YOU.

MAY THE ENEMY DO NOTHING AGAINST HIM, MAY HE NOT DARE TO HARM HIM. SEND HIM, OH LORD, YOUR HELP FROM YOUR HOLY TEMPLE, DEFEND HIM FROM THE HEIGHTS OF YOUR HEAVENLY ABODE. BE FOR HIM LIKE A FORTRESS AGAINST THE ASSAULTS OF THE EVIL ONE.

Lord, hear my prayer.

AND MAY MY CRY REACH YOU.

The Lord be with you.

AND WITH YOUR SPIRIT.

PRAYER

Oh God, who gave the blessed Zeno, your confessor, the power to expel demons from every place, we pray you by his merits and intercession to grant me also the strength to expel these demons who have invaded your creature. For Christ our Lord. Amen.

PRAYER

Oh all you holy angels and archangels, thrones, dominions, principalities and powers, heavenly hosts, cherubim and seraphim who before God ceaselessly lift up your voices saying: Holy, holy, holy is the Lord, God of the universe; send out your holy prayers for me, a frail sinner, to our Lord God, so that he will have mercy on me; forgive my sins, free me, protect me and defend me with his mercy, letting me overcome all my temptations, and thus may he guide me through temporal goods without losing the joy of eternal life. By Christ our Lord. Amen.

PRAYER

Oh supreme Archangel Michael, prince of the heavenly hosts and their illustrious ornament, you who give vigilant service before God, I ask you to intercede with your prayers for me, a miserable mortal, so that, by the mercy of God, he may be freed from every deceit of the devil and by your means I may deserve to be presented before the divine majesty. Amen.

PRAYER

God of angels, God of archangels, God of the prophets, of the apostles, of the martyrs; God of the confessors and virgins, God, Father of our Lord Jesus Christ, I invoke your name and humbly ask for the mercy of your sublime majesty, so that you will deign to help me against this iniquitous spirit. I ask you this through he who will come to judge with fire the living and the dead and the entire world. Amen.

Here, the exorcist rises and recites the following prayer:

Oh God, creator and redeemer of body and soul, favor this creature of yours, [name].

May the soul of Christ ☩ sanctify you. May the glorious body of Christ ☩ save you. May the precious blood of Christ ☩ inebriate you. May the holy sweat of Christ ☩ heal you. May the most bitter passion of Christ ☩ comfort you. May Jesus Christ, the good shepherd, ☩ keep you and free you; may he hide you in his wounds and not permit you to be separated from him; may he defend you from the evil enemy ☩ and free you; in the hour of death, may he call you to go to him, may he place you near him to praise him, together with his angels, forever and ever. Amen.

Here is the cross ☩ of our Lord Jesus Christ, flee, enemy forces, etc.

Lord Jesus Christ, who made heaven and Earth, who blessed the Jordan River in which you wanted to be baptized, deign to bl☩ess and sanctify this creature, [name], you who live and reign with the Father and the Holy Spirit forever and ever. Amen.

Then the following Psalms are read:

Psalm 68:

Let God arise, let his enemies scatter,
Let his opponents flee before him.
You disperse them like smoke;
As wax melts in the presence of a fire,
So the wicked melt in the presence of God.
The upright rejoice in the presence of God,
Delighted and crying out for joy.
Sing to God, play music to his name,
Build a road for the Rider of the Clouds,
Rejoice in Yahweh, dance before him.
Father of orphans, defender of widows,
Such is God in his holy dwelling.
God gives the lonely a home to live in,
Leads prisoners out into prosperity,
But rebels must live in the bare wastelands.
God, when you set out at the head of your people,
When you strode over the desert, the Earth rocked,
The heavens pelted down rain at the presence of God,
At the presence of God, the God of Israel.
God, you rained down a shower of blessings,
When your heritage was weary, you gave it strength.
Your family found a home, which you,
In your generosity, provided for the humble.
The Lord gave a command,
The good news of a countless army.
The chieftains of the army are in flight, in flight,
And the fair one at home is sharing out the spoils.
While you are at ease in the sheepfolds,
The wings of the Dove are being covered with silver,
And her feathers with a sheen of green gold;
When Shaddai scatters the chieftains,
Through her, it snows on the Dark Mountain.
A mountain of God, the mountain of Bashan!
A haughty mountain, the mountain of Bashan!
Why be envious, haughty mountains,
Of the mountain God has chosen for his dwelling?

There, God will dwell for ever.
The chariots of God are thousand upon thousand;
God has come from Sinai to the sanctuary.
You have climbed the heights, taken captives,
You have taken men as tribute, even rebels,
That Yahweh God might have a dwelling-place.
Blessed be the Lord day after day,
He carries us along, God our Saviour.
This God of ours is a God who saves;
From Lord Yahweh comes escape from death;
But God smashes the heads of his enemies,
The long-haired skull of the prowling criminal.
The Lord has said, "I will bring them back from
    Bashan,
I will bring them back from the depths of the sea,
So that you may bathe your feet in blood,
And the tongues of your dogs feast on your
    enemies."
Your processions, God, are for all to see,
The processions of my God, of my king, to the
    sanctuary;
Singers ahead, musicians behind,
In the middle come girls, beating their drums.
In choirs, they bless God,
Yahweh, since the foundation of Israel.
Benjamin was there, the youngest in front,
The princes of Judah in bright-colored robes,
The princes of Zebulun, the princes of Naphtali.
Take command, my God, as befits your power,
The power, God, that you have wielded for us,
From your temple high above Jerusalem.
Kings will come to you bearing tribute.
Rebuke the Beast of the Reeds,
That herd of bulls, that people of calves,
Who bow down with ingots of silver.
Scatter the people who delight in war.

From Egypt, nobles will come,
Ethiopia will stretch out its hands to God.
Kingdoms of the Earth, sing to God,
Play for the Rider of the Heavens, the primeval heavens.
There he speaks, with a voice of power!
Acknowledge the power of God.
Over Israel, his splendor, in the clouds his power.
Awesome is God in his sanctuary.
He, the God of Israel,
Gives strength and power to his people.
Blessed be God.

Psalm 91:

You who live in the secret place of Elyon,
Spend your nights in the shelter of Shaddai,
Saying to Yahweh, "My refuge, my fortress,
My God in whom I trust!"
He rescues you from the snare
Of the fowler set on destruction;
He covers you with his pinions,
You find shelter under his wings.
His constancy is shield and protection.
You need not fear the terrors of night,
The arrow that flies in the daytime,
The plague that stalks in the darkness,
The scourge that wreaks havoc at high noon.
Though a thousand fall at your side,
Ten thousand at your right hand,
You yourself will remain unscathed.
You have only to keep your eyes open
To see how the wicked are repaid,
You who say, "Yahweh, my refuge!"
And make Elyon your fortress.
No disaster can overtake you,
No plague come near your tent;

He has given his angels orders
To guard you wherever you go.
They will carry you in their arms
In case you trip over a stone.
You will walk upon wild beast and adder,
You will trample young lions and snakes.
"Since he clings to me, I rescue him,
I raise him high, since he acknowledges my name.
He calls to me and I answer him:
In distress, I am at his side,
I rescue him and bring him honor.
I shall satisfy him with long life,
And grant him to see my salvation."

After reciting the psalms, the exorcist utters with virile audacity and in a loud voice, with great faith and hope, the following exorcism.

EXORCISM

Most nefarious spirits, rebellious against almighty God, who by your iniquity and as enemies of mankind are destined to end up in the eternal fire, from which you cannot flee in any way; evil traitors, who dared to invade this creature of God, [name], with the authority of our Lord, Jesus Christ, invoking his most holy name, I exhort † you, I exorcise you, I force and oblige you † with the power of God, Fa†ther, S†on, and Holy † Spirit, I order and command you to tell me now, immediately, with no delay, what are your names, why you entered this person, and all your being and all your conditions, with no falsity or deceit. As it is certainly true that in the beginning was the Word and the Word was with God and the Word was God, so in the beginning he was with God: everything was created through him and without him nothing was created. As the aforesaid Word of God, he became flesh, that is, man, true Messiah, a sole person who preached the Gospel of salvation, driving out from the bodies of men unclean spirits and healing the sick; as the same Christ, perfect Word of God, he made himself obedient to the Father till his death on the cross, and after his death, his most holy soul, having left his body on the cross, descended to hell; having defeated the princes of hell, with virile strength he tied up Lucifer and, having exterminated all the power of hell, from there he drew forth the souls of the holy fathers; on the third day, he rose from the dead and, after forty days, he ascended into heaven, and he sits at the right hand of the Father; from there he will come to judge the living and the dead, giving the eternal kingdom to those who are so predestined, while to you reprobates, you rebels against God, he will give the perpetual fire of hell; as, then, all these words are true, so by their power I order you again not to keep silent about your name in any way, nor the reason why you invaded and molest this creature of God, [name].

In the name of Jesus Christ Nazarene, the Crucified, I command you immediately to leave this servant of God with no delay: leave him healthy, as you found him, and never again return. Hurry off to a place where you cannot harm any Christian; I command you by that strength and power with which Lucifer and all the other evil and rebellious angels were cast down from the heavens into hell; and I condemn you in the name of Jesus Christ Nazarene and all his holy names, and I cast you forever into the pool of fire and sulfur. Amen.

Here, the exorcist shall try to find out the names and conditions of the devils that are in the body of the possessed person, forcing them with threats and impositions. Then, he proceeds with the following exorcisms.

EXORCISM

After invoking the name of Christ, I, a sinner, am vested with the authority that the same one, our Lord, gave to the apostles, to their successors, and to all those who believe in him. In fact, he said to his apostles: "I give you power over all the evil spirits and their works." And in a different place, he thus spoke: "These will be the signs accompanying those who believe. In my name they will drive out demons, they will lay their hands on the ill and these will be healed."

In the name of this authority, being (though unworthy) numbered among the faithful, I exhort you, † I contest you, and I exorcise you; with virile strength, I command you, I force you and oblige you, you and all the nefarious spirits who are rebellious against God, unclean and desiring of the eternal fire of hell because of your enormous and shameful crimes; to you, full of pride, rebellion, falsity, abuse, deceit, and filth, I severely command and order by the omnipotence of God the Father, by the wisdom of the Son, by the virtue of the Holy Spirit, by the most holy Trinity, by the immensity, eternity, beauty, nobility, and excellence of God: that all your power and that of any other ally of yours be again tied up. As it is true that he is the God of all, from whom and by whom all things originate, who claims honor and glory, and whom all the powers of the heavens, of the air, and of hell adore and tremble before, thus I order you immediately, with no delay, in the name and by the name of our Lord, Jesus Christ, the crucified Nazarene, to get away from this creature of God, [name], leaving him healthy as you found him. Do not dare to return to him again, and hurry off to a place where you can no longer harm any creature of God. By the same power with which Lucifer and the other evil and rebellious angels were driven out of heaven into hell, in virtue of our Lord, Jesus Christ, the crucified Nazarene, in virtue of the holy names of God, I eternally condemn you and I cast you into the pool that burns with fire and sulfur. Amen.

EXORCISM

Abominable and nefarious spirits, you who with your obstinate rebellion never cease to occupy and molest this creature of god, [name], I command you ☦ by the Fa☦ther, by the S☦on, and by the Holy ☦ Spirit, by means of the holy Mother of God and everything that in the name of Jesus Christ can force you to obey, and I order you immediately to come out and flee from this body, formed by God. Do not dare offend either this creature or me, or any other person. May the ☦ Son of the living God fight against you; he is the origin of every creature. May ☦ Saint Michael Archangel be against you. Against you ☦ Saint Gabriel and ☦ Saint Raphael. May all the powers of the heavens fight against you. In the name of the Fa☦ther, of the S☦on, and of the Holy ☦ Spirit. Amen.

Furthermore, by the power of the Father, of the Son, and of the Holy Spirit, by the authority of our Lord Jesus Christ, by all that I have named before, let Lucifer be against you, that most nefarious spirit, with all the furies and infernal punishments; may he be against you with all his indignation, and furious with wrath; may he rise and attack you; may he immediately strike you and torment you with all the infernal punishments, till the day of judgment, as a cruel minister of God, and according to everything I have said about you. Amen.

EXORCISM

Again and with even greater force and severity, by the authority of our Lord Jesus Christ, the crucified Nazarene, I exorcise you, abominable and hateful spirits, who with your obstinate rebellion do not cease to occupy and molest this creature of God, [name]. By everything I have said before and by everything that in the name of Jesus can make you obey, I command you ✝ by the incarnation, birth, baptism, and holy fasting of Christ; by his passion, death, cross, resurrection, and ascension; by all his holy and blessed life; by the coming of the Holy Spirit paraclete; by Saint John the Baptist, by all the patriarchs and prophets, by the holy fathers of the Old Testament and all their faith, hope, and charity; by their justice, their life, and all the good works that they have performed; by all the Old Testament and all the mysteries therein contained, I order you to get away from this creature of God. Amen.

EXORCISM

Again, I drive you away, oh nefarious and abominable spirits. By the power of God that gives me strength, by God who is admirable, supreme, strong, ineffable and invisible, by these most holy names of God the almighty and by their virtue I command you: the sacred Tetragram, ✝ Elohim, ✝ Adonai, ✝ Immanuel, ✝ Messiah, ✝ Hagios, ✝ ho Theòs, ✝ Ischyròs, ✝ Athanatos, ✝ Sabaoth, ✝ King, ✝ Judge, ✝ Guide, ✝ Light, ✝ Legislator, ✝ Father, ✝ Master, ✝ Beginning, ✝ Word, ✝ Consubstantial, ✝ Alpha and Omega, ✝ Image, ✝ Wisdom, ✝ Door, ✝ Way, ✝ Life, ✝ Morning Star, ✝ Prophet, ✝ Rock, ✝ Vine, ✝ Key, ✝ Virtue, ✝ Firstborn, ✝ Most High, ✝ Lamb, ✝ Sheep, ✝ Husband, ✝ First and Last, ✝ Creator, ✝ Redeemer, ✝ Shepherd, ✝ Splendor, ✝ Teacher, ✝ Sun, ✝ Flower, ✝ Priest, ✝ Pontifex, ✝ Truth, ✝ Charity, ✝ only-begotten, ✝ Fountain, ✝ Paraclete, ✝ Mediator, ✝ Jesus, ✝ Lord, ✝ God ✝ Almighty, and ✝ Eternal.

✝ By virtue of the most holy name of God, YHWH, by all his other names, by all the exorcisms, exhortations, commands, and impositions of any kind with which, in the name of Jesus Christ, you can be driven out, forced, tied and set fleeing, or sent from one place to another, or else tormented and subjected to pain and punishment, by all this may every place on Earth be immediately forbidden you, except the center of the Earth. And I, as minister of Christ, cast you into the pool of fire and sulfur and condemn you eternally to remain there. I curse you; I throw you and bind you to the depths of the abyss till the day of judgment. May you thus be subject to all the infernal punishments, more harsh and painful than those of Lucifer, for you were rebellious toward such great and numerous names and divine mysteries. By virtue of all those I uttered before, I order you to immediately get away from this creature of God, [name], in the manner and in the conditions that I have said and commanded. From this instant and forever in the future, by force of what I have declared and in the name and by virtue of our Lord, Jesus Christ, may every power of yours be tied up, like that of anyone favoring you, and may you never again be able to resist against my orders—or rather the orders of Christ, by whose authority I exercise this office (though not through my merit). Christ himself then orders you this, he who voluntarily let himself be tied to the column and nailed to the cross. Amen.

And if the devil does not want to listen or obey, take fire and sulfur, and make their smoke smolder over the possessed person, whether he likes it or not, until he tells the truth about what you desire to know.

EXORCISM

Again I drive you away, ✝ spirits rebellious against God, to whom power has been given over this body and over all the human bodies tormented by you. I command you by the Fa✝ther, the S✝on, and the Holy ✝ Spirit immediately to go away from this person. I exhort you ✝ and I order you by all the holy virgins and penitents. I exorcise you ✝ and order you by Saint Mary Magdalene, Catherine, Agnes, Lucy, Agatha, Marguerite, Dorothy, Ursula and her companions; by Anne, Elizabeth, and all the other virgins and widows and penitent women, I order you to go out of this person. Again I drive you out, ✝ spirits rebellious against God, by the most blessed Virgin Mary, mother of our Lord Jesus Christ, ✝ by her nativity, ✝ by her virginity, ✝ by her conception, ✝ by her holy milk that was sucked by the mouth of the one called Alpha and Omega, ✝ Yah, ✝ Shaddai, ✝ Immanuel, ✝ Tetragram; ✝ by his merits, by all the good things that can be said and thought of the most blessed Virgin Mary, and by all the names with which she is invoked: Virgin, ✝ Flower, ✝ Cloud, ✝ Queen, ✝ Theotokos, ✝ Empress, ✝ Lady, ✝ Sunrise, ✝ Handmaiden, ✝ Garden, ✝ Fountain, ✝ Well, ✝ Hall, ✝ Thornbush, ✝ Ladder, ✝ Star, ✝ Tower, ✝ Help, ✝ Ark, ✝ Marriage Bed, ✝ Precious Pearl, ✝ Tabernacle, ✝ Friend, ✝ Veil, ✝ All Beautiful, ✝ Mother, ✝ Soul, ✝ Lovely, ✝ Fine, ✝ Blessed, ✝ Bride, ✝ Mary. By all these names that I have said, I command you and cast you into the pool of fire and I condemn you eternally. And just as the blessed Virgin Mary and the other virgins, widows, and penitent saints enjoy eternal glory with Christ, so you, in this instant, in the name of Jesus Christ our Lord, the crucified Nazarene, by virtue of his passion, must immediately go away from this creature of God, [name], in the manner and conditions that I ordered before. Otherwise, by what I have mentioned, be condemned forever to that inextinguishable pain and torment, expressly destined to you as rebels against God. Amen.

EXORCISM

Again I drive you out ✝ with greater force and severity, oh nefarious and abominable spirits, who do not cease to molest this creature of God with your obstinate rebellion. By all I have said before, and by the things that can set you fleeing, by the authority of our Lord Jesus Christ, the crucified Nazarene, I drive you away, I oppose you, I exorcise you. With virile force, I order you, I command and force you by all the angels, the archangels, thrones, dominions, principalities and powers, the heavenly hosts, the cherubim and seraphim, of whose glory and company you have justly been forever deprived because of your crimes. By the most holy names of the angels of God, Michael, Gabriel, and Raphael, and by all the other names of angels, I order you immediately to go away with no delay. As you and the other reprobates have justly been forever deprived of the glory and company of the aforesaid holy angels, and have been condemned to the punishments of hell; as the elect and the predestined will enjoy the eternal glory of God together with the aforesaid angels, while you will be tormented for your fault in the eternal fire together with Lucifer and all those subject to the infernal punishments, thus I order you, immediately and without delay to go away from this creature of God, [name], since you have been conquered and driven away by the authority and power of our Lord, Jesus Christ, the crucified Nazarene. I order you to go into the wilderness, where you cannot harm any creature, with no further delay or pretext. Leave this creature of God whom you have been tormenting for so long; leave him with the good health he once had, and do not come back to molest him. Otherwise, by virtue of the Fa✝ther, of the S✝on, and of the Holy ✝ Spirit, by the authority of our Lord Jesus Christ, by what I have already said, may Lucifer himself rise up against you, that nefarious spirit, together with all his vassals and all the furies and infernal punishments, with all his indignation and wrath, and may he come down upon you and drag you into the pool of fire and sulfur, into the depths of the abyss till the day of judgment. In fact, he operates as a cruel minister of God, and there he will torment

you harshly with all the punishments of hell, by everything
that has been said. Amen.

EXORCISM

Again, I drive you away, ✝ hateful spirits, rebellious against
God, by the names and by the mysteries of God, by the
authority of our Lord Jesus Christ, the crucified Nazarene,
and I command you severely by all the holy pontifices, doctors, confessors, monks and hermits, priests and Levites,
that is, by Saints Gregory, Ambrose, Ciprianus,
Geminianus, Bernardino, Francis, Dominic, Paul, the first
hermit Anthony, and the blessed Nicholas of Tolentino; by
all their blessed lives, by all their merits, prayers, and good
works. And just as the angel tied up the writhing serpent,
thus may all your power and that of your allies be tied up
by means of these most holy names of the Son of God and
by their virtue, for he is the ✝ Firstborn, ✝ Wisdom, ✝
Force, ✝ Sun, ✝ Splendor, ✝ Light, ✝ Glory, ✝ Bread, ✝
Spring, ✝ Salvation, ✝ Mountain, ✝ Door, ✝ Stone, ✝
Word, ✝ Husband, ✝ Shepherd, ✝ Prophet, ✝ Mediator,
✝ Lamb, ✝ Sheep, ✝ Vine, ✝ Truth, ✝ Way, ✝ Lion, ✝
Light from light. ✝ As all the saints that we have named
rejoice together in the presence of Christ, so I order you
immediately to go away from this creature of God, [name],
in the manner and condition that I imposed before.
Otherwise, with all the severity and power that come to me
from the authority of Christ the Lord, from this moment
on, I command and order Lucifer and all the infernal furies
immediately and instantly to rise against you, so that they
may lead you to the pool of fire and sulfur, into the depths
of the abyss, and there tie you up and torment you with all
the punishments, so that none of you who rebel against
God and his saints can be free of these punishments till the
day of judgment. In the name of the Fa✝ther, of the S✝on,
and of the Holy ✝ Spirit. Amen.

Fourth Exorcism
TERRIBLE AND OF GREAT EFFICACY AGAINST DEVILS WHO OPPRESS HUMAN BODIES

After taking part in the sacrament of confession, the exorcist who is about to perform the exorcism, with a pure and devout heart, kneeling before the image of the Crucifix, shall recite Psalm 51 :

Have mercy on me, O God, in your faithful love. . .

Of hidden sins, purify me, oh Lord.

AND PROTECT YOUR SERVANT FROM PRIDE.

Lord, hear my prayer.

AND MAY MY CRY REACH YOU.

The Lord be with you.

AND WITH YOUR SPIRIT.

PRAYER

Oh God, who manifests yourself in mercy and forgiveness, accept our invocation and, in the clemency of your pity, absolve me, your servant, oppressed by the chain of his crimes. Through Christ, our Lord. Amen.

PRAYER

Oh God, who gave your holy apostles the power to drive out demons from every place, we supplicate you to grant that, through their merits and their intercession, I may receive the strength to drive out these demons who oppress your servant [name]. You who live and reign with the Father and the Holy Spirit forever and ever. Amen.

PRAYER

God of heaven, God of the Earth, God of the angels and archangels, God of the patriarchs and prophets, God of the apostles, of the martyrs, of confessors and of virgins, God of all the living; God, whom every tongue acknowledges and before whom every knee bends in heaven, on Earth, and in hell; God, who has the power to give life after death and rest after toil; there is no God but you and, truly, there cannot be another God wherever you perform your work; and your kingdom is everlasting. Now, I humbly invoke you, Lord, my God, and I humbly supplicate your glorious majesty, that, without considering my countless sins and those of this creature, but only through your mercy, you might wish to liberate this servant of yours, [name], from unclean spirits, and lead him to the grace of true liberation.

Oh truly eternal God, who are the God of Abraham, Isaac, and Jacob, the God of Moses, of Aaron, Tobias, and Elias; I humbly invoke you, almighty and eternal god, that you might command and allow liberation of your servant from the temptations of unclean spirits. From the beginning, these unclean spirits were fallacious and never stood on the side of truth, but always, with the maliciousness of their iniquity, pride, vanity, and greed, assist those who oppress with insults and molestation your servant [name]. Oh Lord God, also command your benign angels to destroy and cast into the depths of the abyss your malignant enemies. May these ancient and cruel serpents, always ready to devour, lose their strength and immediately be set fleeing, together with their allies. As in your wrath and your furor, Lord, you destroyed Sodom and Gomorra, so command the striking of all your malignant enemies and adversaries who vex, haunt, and wish to deceive this servant of yours, [name]. Let them not be able to hide in his body without being manifested; and let them not find any instrument of evildoing, even in any garment or part of his body. May they not be able to occupy that body that you, Lord, formed on Earth, giving it bones, nerves, and spirit. Through the glory of your name, Lord, through the name of your Son, Jesus Christ, and through the power of his cross, let them be dispersed like straw at the puff of the wind; as smoke ceases, so may they fail and perish. May all demons be dispersed from the soul and body of your servant [name] and may they end up in arid wilderness, where no saint or just man lives. We ask you all this because you, Lord, did not ransom us with gold and silver, but with your precious blood and your most holy body; with your passion you redeemed us, oh Jesus Christ, savior of the world. May the angels praise you, to you be given praise and glory forever. Amen.

Rising from prayer, here the exorcist reads the following passage from the Gospel.

From the Gospel according to Mark (5:1–20):

They reached the territory of the Gerasenes on the other side of the lake, and when he disembarked, a

man with an unclean spirit at once came out from
the tombs toward him. The man lived in the tombs
and no one could secure him any more, even with a
chain, because he had often been secured with fetters and chains, but had snapped the chains and broken the fetters, and no one had the strength to
control him. All night and all day, among the tombs
and in the mountains, he would howl and gash himself with stones. Catching sight of Jesus from a dis-
tance, he ran up and fell at his feet and shouted at
the top of his voice, "What do you want with me,
Jesus, Son of the Most High God? In God's name,
do not torture me!" for Jesus had been saying to
him, "Come out of the man, unclean spirit." Then
he asked, "What is your name?" He answered, "My
name is Legion, for there are many of us." And he
begged him earnestly not to send them out of the
district. Now on the mountainside, there was a great
herd of pigs feeding, and the unclean spirits begged
him, "Send us to the pigs, let us go into them." So
he gave them leave. With that, the unclean spirits
came out and went into the pigs, and the herd of
about two thousand pigs charged down the cliff into
the lake, and there they were drowned. The men
looking after them ran off and told the story in the
city and in the country round about; and the people
came to see what had really happened. They came to
Jesus and saw the demoniac sitting there—the man
who had had the legion in him—properly dressed
and in his full senses, and they were afraid. And
those who had witnessed it reported what had happened to the demoniac and what had become of the
pigs. Then they began to implore Jesus to leave their
neighborhood. As he was getting into the boat, the
man who had been possessed begged to be allowed
to stay with him. Jesus would not let him, but said

to him, "Go home to your people and tell them all the Lord in his mercy has done for you." So the man went off and proceeded to proclaim in the Decapolis all that Jesus had done for him. And everyone was amazed.

PRAISE TO YOU, OH CHRIST.

After the reading, the exorcist shall approach the possessed person and, making a sign on his forehead, shall say:

El, ✝ Elohim, ✝ Eloah, ✝ Eheye, ✝ sacred Tetragram, ✝ Adonai, ✝ Shaddai, ✝ Sabaoth, ✝ Soter, ✝ Immanuel, ✝ Alpha and Omega, ✝ First and Last, ✝ Beginning and End, ✝ Hagios, ✝ Ischyròs, ✝ ho Theòs, ✝ Athànatos, ✝ Agla, ✝ Jehova, ✝ Homousios, ✝ Yah.

✝ Christ wins, ✝ Christ reigns, ✝ Christ rules. ✝ Non-created the Father, ✝ non-created the Son, ✝ non-created the Holy Spirit.

✝ Jesus ✝ Christ, our God, ✝by the sign of the ✝ cross free us from our enemies.

EXORCISM

I exhort ✝ you and I command you, I contest you and I exorcise you through the non-created divinity, the immensity, the eternity, the glory, the immortal, impassible, immutable, incomprehensible majesty; through the power, justice, mercy, wisdom, beauty, clemency, benignity, kindness, sanctity, grace, and influence of the living and almighty God, who gives me strength and whom all creatures obey. Through the marvelous divine preordination, by which God, from eternity, decided to send his Son, Jesus Christ, to save the world, again I exhort you ✝ and I command you, I contest you and exorcise you by the only Father, the only Son, the only Holy Spirit; by the Trinity that is one, by the unity in trinity, by the only mystery in the incarnation of the Word, by the only Almighty, the only eternal, the only immortal, the only impassible, the only incomprehensible, the only incorruptible, the only one who created every being; by the only nativity of Christ in the flesh, by his only circumcision, by the only baptism, by the death of Christ which is one alone, by his only descent into hell, by the only resurrection of Christ and his ascension into heaven; by the only orthodox Church, the only Catholic faith, the only last day, by the only cross of Christ, I command you to come out without delay from this creature of God, [name], in the manner and condition I indicated above, bringing no harm to him or to any other Christian. Act in such a way that I can know the things I wish to know, otherwise, through all that I have said before, with supreme severity and power, by the authority of our Lord, Jesus Christ, the crucified Nazarene, I order and command Lucifer and all the infernal furies to rise up against you immediately and at once; may they assault you and make you fall into the pool of fire and sulfur, and may they tie you up and torment you pitilessly in the depths of the abyss. Amen.

EXORCISM

Again I exorcise you ✝ and I drive you out, oh spirits, by all that I have already said and by everything that can set you fleeing, by the authority of our Lord, Jesus Christ, the crucified Nazarene. Abominable and nefarious spirits, who insist in your rebellion, and haunt and oppress this creature of God, I chain you up in such a way that you cannot be freed, by the majesty of him whom the Sun and Moon admire for his beauty. May the wrath of the Lord descend upon you. I exhort ✝ you by the most holy Trinity, Fa✝ther, S✝on, and Holy ✝ Spirit; by the power, ✝ wisdom, ✝ commandment, and unity of the living and

almighty God and our Lord, Jesus Christ: by his annunciation, ✝his circumcision, ✝ his holy baptism, ✝ his preaching; ✝ by his doctrine ✝ and his pains, ✝ by the cross ✝
on which he was crucified, ✝ by the nails that fixed him to
it, ✝ by the crown of thorns that he wore upon his head, ✝
by the spear that rent his side, ✝ by the blood and water
that came forth from it, ✝ by his holy words written on the
cross, that is, Jesus the Nazarene, King of the Jews.

I exorcise you ✝ by the death of Christ and by his resurrection, by his apparitions, by his holy body, by his soul
and his spirit, by all the good works performed by him and
by everything that can be said and thought about the
Creator of all creatures; by the tremendous day of judgment, I order you to get away from this creature of God,
[name], with no harm to him or any other Christian. In the
name of the Fa✝ther, of the S✝on, and of the Holy ✝
Spirit. Amen.

*Here, the exorcist takes the blessed herb-of-grace and, with
the proper formula given below, and placing it under the
nostrils of the possessed person, recites the following exorcism:*

EXORCISM

I exorcise you, ✝ I drive you out and I contest you by that
same Lord whom you tempted on the mountain, saying to
him: "If you are the Son of God, throw yourself down and
change these stones into bread." I exorcise you ✝ and I
drive you out by the same person who answered you:
"Away with you, Satan, do not put the Lord God to the
test, but do him homage, him alone you must serve." I drive
you out ✝ by all the apostles of Christ, I drive you out ✝
by means of all the martyrs of Christ, ✝ by all the confessors, ✝ the ✝ virgins, and ✝ by all the ministers of Christ.
I drive you out ✝ by means of the Crucified One who saves

us, ✝ by Michael, Gabriel, and Raphael. I drive you out ✝ by the tremendous day of judgment, ✝ by the resurrection of the savior, ✝ by the patriarch, the prophet, and ✝ by the prince of the apostles, Saint Peter. Amen.

Insults against the devils

I drive you out ✝ by the God of Abraham, of Isaac and Jacob, by the cross ✝ of the Lord, by the Fa✝ther, the S✝on, and the Holy ✝ Spirit. Unclean spirit, miserable tempter, deceiver, father of lies, heretic, fool, beastly, furious enemy of your Creator, lascivious serpent and dried-up pig, starving and unclean beast full of rust, scabby and truculent beast, most beastly beast of all, driven from Paradise and from the ineffable place, deprived of the grace of God, of the communion and company of angels, accursed creature, reprobate, damned by God eternally for your pride and malignity, evil, nefarious, accursed, excommunicated, blasphemous, damned and damning, no longer inhabit this creature of God, [name]. Amen.

EXORCISM

I drive you away, ✝ evil spirit, on behalf of the holy Mother of God and ever-Virgin Mary, and in the name of her most beloved son; by the blessed milk with which she nourished him, by the blessed veil in which she wrapped him: get away, evil spirit, with all your companions, from this creature of God, [name]. I drive you out ✝ by the Father, the Son, and the Holy Spirit, by the Holy Trinity, by the inviolate Mother of God, Mary, by the names of God, Alpha and Omega, First and Last, Beginning and End, Immanuel, Adonai, and the great name Sabaoth. I drive you away ✝ by the incarnation and nativity of God. I exorcise you ✝ by the angels and the archangels, thrones, dominions, principalities and powers, heavenly hosts, cherubim and

seraphim, apostles and evangelists; by all the holy
Innocents, by the martyrs and confessors, the virgins and
widows, by all the saints of God. I drive you away ✝ by
the Son of the living God, who was hung up on the cross
for us sinners and will come to judge with fire the living and
the dead and the entire universe. I exorcise you ✝ by Saints
Matthew, Mark, Luke, and John, by the eleven thousand
virgins, for Christ wins, Christ reigns, Christ rules. I drive
you out ✝ by the goodness of Christ, ✝ by his annunciation, ✝ by the apparition, circumcision, and baptism of Christ,
✝ by his miracles, ✝ by his temptation, ✝ by the humility
with which he washed the feet of his disciples, ✝ by the passion of Christ, ✝ the crown of thorns, ✝ by the vinegar
given him to drink, ✝ by the spear that pierced him, ✝ by
the blood and water that came out from his side, ✝ by the
invocation that Christ made while hanging from the cross,
saying: "*Eli, Eli, lemà sabactani*"; by the tomb of Christ, ✝
by the winding cloth that wrapped his body, ✝ by the
power with which Christ rose from the dead, ✝ by all
the heavenly assembly, by the virtue of all the saints, I order
✝ and command you immediately to come out of this creature of God, [name], doing him no harm, and to act in such
a way that I can know the truth. In the name of the Father,
✝ of the Son, ✝and of the Holy Spirit. Amen.

EXORCISM

Now, accursed devil, recognize your sentence, know the
sentence of just condemnation for your iniquity and,
though recalcitrant and forced to act against your
malignant will, render honor to the living and true ✝ God,
render honor to his Son and our Lord, Jesus Christ, ✝ render honor to the Holy ✝ Spirit paraclete: come out and
withdraw from this creature of God, [name], for our God
and Lord, Jesus Christ, has deigned to call him to his grace;
and do not dare to violate this sign of the holy cross, ✝

which we make on your forehead, oh accursed devil, but get away, for you have been exorcised by he who will come to judge with fire the living and the dead and the entire world, and you as well, oh devil, enemy of mankind. In the name of the Father, ✝ of the Son, ✝ and of the Holy ✝ Spirit. Amen.

Here, he asks questions about the name, companions, departure, and all other things regarding the liberation of the possessed person. Then he continues in this manner.

EXORCISM

Again, with greater force and severity, I exhort you, ✝ I order you, I exorcise you, I command and oblige you to get away, all of you filthy spirits, nefarious and rebellious against God, worthy of eternal fire because of your immense and abominable crimes. To you who are full of all pride, rebellion, falsity, and abuse, full of filth and deceit, I command and order by the mighty and fortifying name of El, strong and wondrous God; I command you by he who spoke, and all things were created, and by all his names. I exorcise you ✝ by means of he who liberated Noah with all his family from the waters of the flood. I exorcise you ✝ by means of he who freed Isaac from being killed by the hand of Abraham his father. I exorcise you, ✝ spirits rebellious against God, and I command you with the courage of he who fought against Jacob and then freed him from the hand of his brother, Esau. I drive you away ✝ and I command you, spirits rebellious against God, with the force of the holy God, whom Moses heard on Mount Oreb, deserving to speak to him and hear him speak in the burning bush. I exorcise you ✝ by means of him whom Moses called by name and all the waters of the rivers and swamps of Egypt became blood and rotted. I exorcise you ✝ in the name of him whom Moses invoked and all the rivers boiled, so that the frogs went up into the houses of the Egyptians, devouring everything. I exorcise you ✝ by means of him whom Moses called by name, striking the dust of the Earth, and the mosquitoes came to molest and assault all the animals of Egypt. I drive you away ✝ in the name of him whom Moses invoked and a grave pestilence struck all the donkeys, the oxen, and camels, killing them. I drive you away ✝ by that God who ordered Moses to take ashes and scatter them in the air, and thus the men and animals in the fields fell dead. I ✝ exorcise you in the name of him whom Moses invoked and the locusts came over the face of the Earth to devour what the hail had not destroyed. I drive you away in the name of him whom Moses invoked and horrible darkness was made for three days and three nights; and for him whom Moses called by name and all the firstborn of Egypt died. I exorcise you ✝ in the name of him whom Moses invoked and all the people of Israel were liberated from slavery by the powerful hand.

EXORCISM

I exhort you, ✝ and I exorcise you, I contest and drive you away, I command with force, oh spirits rebellious against God, by means of him whom Moses called by name and the sea obeyed him and divided, while all the chariots of Pharaoh were destroyed. I drive you away by that same power ✝ that made copious waters spring from the rock. I exorcise you ✝ by him whom Moses heard on Mount Sinai and deserved to receive the tables written by his hand. I drive you away ✝ and I exorcise you and I command you with virile force, spirits rebellious against God, by means of he who gave Joshua victory as he fought against his enemies; by him whom the holy King David invoked, and was liberated from the hands of Goliath. I drive you away ✝ by means of him to whom the prophet Elijah prayed not to make rain, and for three years and six months it did not rain on the face of the Earth; then he again prayed so that it would rain, and the sky sent rain and the Earth bore fruit. I exorcise you ✝ by means of him whom Elisha named, and the Sunamite had a son; by he who foretold to Jeremiah his deportation to Jerusalem and by he who gave Daniel the force to destroy Baal and to kill the dragon. I drive you out ✝ in the name of him whom the three youths invoked in the burning furnace and they were liberated, totally unharmed. By all the names of the living and true God, God almighty, who, through your fault expelled you from heaven and from his supreme throne, I, too, on his behalf, cast you down and condemn you to the infernal abyss. Amen.

EXORCISM

I exhort you, ✝ I contest you and I exorcise you, I drive you away and command you with force, oh spirits rebellious to God, by means of he who spoke and things were created; by means of him whom all creatures obey; by the tremendous day of judgment of God; by the four animals that are around the throne of God and have eyes in front and back; by the holy eternity that God possesses and by the names that are given to the Son of God; by the ineffable power of the Creator, by the supreme wisdom of the Almighty; by the most holy name of Jesus, before which every creature fears and trembles. By the nine choirs of the angels, I command you to speak with me immediately and with no deceit or falsity, without noisiness, without lying or injury, but obeying my commands and diligently fulfilling what I order. As by the name of God that Moses invoked, Dathan and Abiram were swallowed up in the pits of the Earth, so by the force of that most holy name, I curse you and cast you down and relegate you to the depths of the abyss till judgment day. Amen.

Here, the exorcist shall use incense blessed by himself and, throwing it into the fire blessed by him as well, shall say this:

PRAYER

Oh Adonai, Shaddai, Elohim, by the invocation of your most holy name, oh holy Lord, Father almighty, eternal God, bring us your succor upon the smoke of this incense, so that we may be helped in expelling these accursed spirits who imprison this creature made in your image and resemblance. As the smoke of the aromas rises before you, Lord Jesus Christ, thus may the smoke of this incense torment, inflame, and send away these nefarious and abominable spirits. By all the heavenly hosts, let these evil spirits have no more power over this creature [name], redeemed by your precious blood. You who live and reign forever and ever. Amen.

EXORCISM

Again I exhort you ✝ by means of the power of God who gives me strength, and I command you, spirits rebellious to God, by him whom Enoch and Elijah invoked in order to struggle against the Antichrist; by he who, on the holy mountain, will put an end to the vices of all the Earth; by he who, announced by the trumpet of the angels having that office, will call the world to terrible judgment. I drive you away ✝ by means of he who makes the angels cry out: "Rise, oh dead, and come to judgment." At the sound of their voices, all the dead, good and bad, will rise in the blinking of an eye. I drive you away by means of he who resurrects the just and immediately, the angels carry them to heaven, so that they will reign forever with the Lord. I drive you away by he who resurrects all those who received the spirit of life in the fullness of Christ. I drive you away ✝ by he who, with the same material, will re-form that same body, giving it all integrity and decorum, for God will recompose in its just place each body or member, even if dispersed. I exorcise you by means of him before whom every mountain will be leveled, every cliff become a plateau, every escarpment a plain. I exorcise you by him upon whose arrival the stars will darken and fall from the sky. I drive you away by he who will come to judge everything. As the emperor, when he is about to enter a city wearing a crown on his head, has all the standards to which he is entitled borne in so that his arrival will be made known, thus the Lord will come to judge the world surrounded by all the hosts of his angels. When the angels are seen to advance, all things will be overwhelmed by a tempest of fire and enormous strokes of lightning that will fall everywhere, as is written in the psalm: "Before him walks fire, burning his enemies all around." Then, all the land will fight on the side of the Lord against fools and, after terminating the judgment, with force and power, God himself will cast the devil and his allies into prison and into the pool of fire and sulfur, while, together with all his chosen, he will return to the celestial homeland in triumphant glory.

EXORCISM

I exorcise you, ✝ spirits rebellious to God, with the same power with which God once let the waters of the flood fall down upon the Earth, and the mountains were covered with fifteen cubits of water. So will God make burning fire come upon the face of the Earth. I exorcise you, ✝ I confront you, I drive you out and command you with force, rebellious spirits, in the name of the living God, true and holy, by the almightiness with which he will transform the purified world and will make it last forever, as the psalm says: "Like a robe you shall change them and they shall pass." I exorcise you ✝ and I command you, I force you with power by all the terrible names of God and by the works that I remembered before and that he shall perform; by his most holy seat and by the beatitude in which he gloriously lives, reigns, governs, and will reign forever and ever. Amen.

EXORCISM

Again I exorcise you, spirits rebellious to God, by the holy names of Elohim and ✝ Eloah, ✝ so that you will immediately respond, obeying my commands, and get away without delay. Otherwise, by virtue of the holy names of God, I cast you into the pool of fire and sulfur and condemn you forever. Amen.

I exorcise you, ✝ rebellious spirits, by the most powerful God who assists me, by the strong, wondrous, and invisible God, by these four holy names of God, Tetragram, ✝ Alpha and Omega, ✝ Jahveh, ✝ and Agla, ✝ so that you will respond and obey me, getting away with no delay. Otherwise, in virtue of the holy names of God, I cast you down to burn eternally in the pool of fire and sulfur, and I condemn you till the day of judgment. Amen.

I exorcise you ✝ and I command you by our Lord God, who, through the mouths of the prophets, said: "It is I who deal death and life; when I have struck, it is I who heal (no one can rescue anyone from me)" (Deut. 32:39). Immediately get away in the way and manner I have told you before, otherwise, by the force and virtue of the holy names of God, I condemn you as it was sentenced against you before. I drive you away ✝ by the grace of the Holy Spirit paraclete and by the obedience of Isaac, who was obedient to his father until death: immediately respond, obeying without delay whatever I command, otherwise, in force of the holy names of God, I cast you down to burn eternally in the pool of fire and sulfur and I condemn you till the day of judgment. Amen.

I exorcise you ✝ by the three youths, Sadrach, Mesach, and Abdeneg, who were cast into the burning furnace and did not die; by the names of Christ, by the tremendous day of judgment, by the ineffable God, creator of all things; by the seven candelabra that are on the right hand of God, by the sweat and blood of Christ; by the angels, the

archangels, the thrones, dominions, principalities and powers, the hosts of cherubim and seraphim; by the death and
burial of Christ, immediately get away from this creature
of God, [name]. I exorcise you ✝ O spirits rebellious to
God, by the suffrage of the prophets, by the merits of the
apostles, by the victory of the martyrs, by the faith of the
confessors, by the chastity of the virgins, by the intercession
of all the saints and chosen of God, so that you will immediately leave this creature of God, [name]. I exorcise you, ✝
evil spirits, and I command you; I exorcise you without
ceasing and with power I drive you away; with virile
courage, I command you to go away, by the circumcision
and the holy fast of Christ, by his baptism, by the passion,
resurrection, and ascension into heaven of our Lord, Jesus
Christ; by his burial, by the bread that he broke and gave
to his disciples at the Last Supper, saying: "Take this and
eat. This is my body." And by the wine that he poured into
the chalice, saying: "Take this and drink, each one of you:
this is the blood of the new covenant, which will be shed for
you in remission of sins." And by that ardent love that the
Virgin Mary bore for Jesus Christ, and by the bond of favor
tying Christ to the Church, I order you to get away immediately, from this creature of God, [name].

EXORCISM

I exorcise you, ✝ spirits rebellious to God, who have
received power over this body and over all others who are
vexed by you, and I order you, through the Fa✝ther, the
S✝on, and the Holy ✝ Spirit, by all the holy apostles of
God, the cardinals, bishops, presbyters, deacons, sub-dea-
cons, acolytes, exorcists, host-bearers and lectors, by the
great name of God, El ✝; answer me and obey according to
what I command you, acting with care; immediately get
away from this creature of God, [name], otherwise, in
virtue and by means of the holy names of God, I cast you

into the pool of fire and sulfur, so that you will burn eternally. Till the day of judgment, I condemn you and immediately, without delay, as conquered and defeated ones, by the authority and power of our Lord, Jesus Christ, come out of this creature of God, [name], doing no harm to him nor to other Christians, and act in such a way that I can know the truth [about your departure]. Withdraw into the wilderness, where you can no longer molest any creature. Immediately leave this creature of God whom you have been molesting for so long; let him regain his former state of health, and may you no longer injure him. In the name of the Fa✝ther, the S✝on, and the Holy ✝ Spirit. Amen.

FIFTH EXORCISM
AGAINST UNCLEAN SPIRITS

Dressed in sacred robes, the exorcist shall go toward the altar or before some holy image; after taking part in the sacrament of confession (as said several times before), with a firm and humble heart, kneeling and making the sign of the cross, he shall say the following prayers:

In the name of the most holy and undivided Trinity, Fa✝ther, S✝on, and Holy ✝ Spirit. Amen.

Our help is in the name of the Lord.

HE MADE HEAVEN AND EARTH.

Show us your mercy, Lord.

AND GIVE US YOUR SALVATION.

Help us, oh God our salvation.

AND BY THE GLORY OF YOUR NAME FREE US, LORD.

May the enemy have no power over us.

AND MAY THE SON OF INIQUITY NOT SUCCEED IN HARMING US.

May your mercy be upon us, Lord.

FOR WE HAVE PUT OUR HOPES IN YOU.

Rise, oh Christ, and help us.

BY YOUR NAME, FREE US.

Lord, hear my prayer.

AND MAY MY CRY REACH YOU.

The Lord be with you.

AND WITH YOUR SPIRIT.

PRAYER

Lord Jesus Christ, who gave to your apostles force and power over the infirm and the weak, so as to heal the sick, resurrect the dead, clean the lepers, drive out demons; confirm in me this grace, though I am an unworthy and miserable sinner: do not consider my countless sins. You who tend to show mercy to sinners and answer the prayers of the humble, by your great goodness now deign to answer me; as you answered the thief upon the cross, so now answer me, I who invoke you in the struggle against this spirit who oppresses your servant [name]. By your holy and terrible name, render me capable of driving him away. You who live and reign with the Father and the Holy Spirit forever and ever. Amen.

Rising from prayer, the exorcist here reads the following passages from the gospels:

John 1:1–14:

In the beginning was the Word. . .

Mark 16:14–20:

While they were at table he reproached them for their incredulity. . .

Matthew 4:1–11:

Then Jesus was led by the Spirit out into the desert to be put to the test by the devil. . .

Then he recites the following words, making the sign of the cross on the forehead of the possessed person.

El, ✝ Elohim, ✝ Eloah, ✝Eheye, ✝ Tetragram (holy), ✝Adonai, ✝ Sabaoth, ✝ Messiah, ✝ Soter, ✝ Immanuel, ✝ Hagios, ✝ Ischyros, ✝ ho Theos, ✝ Athànatos, ✝ Agla, ✝ Jehovah, ✝Yah; ✝ Christ conquers, ✝ Christ reigns, ✝ Christ governs. Non-created the Father, ✝ non-created the Son, ✝ non-created the Holy Spirit. ✝ Here is the cross ✝ of the Lord, flee enemy forces: the lion of the tribe of Judah has won, the holy root of David is victorious.

EXORCISM

I drive you away, ✝ spirits rebellious to God, who, with your obstinate rebellion, continue to possess and molest this creature of God, [name]; I exorcise you with every means with which, in the name of Jesus, one can command and force, and in particular by means of the Fa✝ther, of the S✝on, and of the Holy ✝ Spirit, which sits on its sublime throne and reigns over everything, arranging each thing with virtue and power. I exorcise you ✝ by the powerful and luminous name of God, El, and by the same God that sits on his supreme throne, one God alone in essence and three in person, on whom all things depend, both in their origin and in their preservation, for he is the Creator and preserver of all. I exorcise you † by all the glory and omnipotence of his divine majesty; by the four animals surrounding his throne, by the seat of divine majesty and by the seven golden candelabra that are before the throne of God; by the twenty-four elders who sit before God and who, each day, ceaselessly acclaim: Holy, holy, holy is the Lord God Sabaoth. I then order you immediately and without delay to go away from this creature of God, [name], like wax melting before the fire. Otherwise, in virtue of God the Father, Son, and Holy Spirit, with the authority of our Lord, Jesus Christ, the crucified Nazarene, by everything I have said, let the most nefarious spirit of Lucifer rise up against you, with all his subjects and all the infernal furies and punishments; may he himself, in all his wrath and indignation, immediately sink you into the pool of fire and sulfur and, as the cruel minister of God, may he torment you with all the punishments of hell till the day of judgment, forever and ever. Amen.

EXORCISM

Again I exorcise you, † spirits rebellious to God, by these most holy names of God. El, † Elohim, † Eloah, † Adonai, † Shaddai, † Light, † holy Tetragram, † Alpha and Omega, † Messiah, † Soter, † Immanuel, † Sabaoth, † Wisdom, † Power, † Way, † Truth, † Life, † Hagios, † ho Theòs, † Ischyròs, † Athànatos, † Beginning and End, † and by all the other names of God, known and unknown; by both mortal and immortal creatures, I order you not to oppress any longer, and not to be able to oppress or injure or molest or torment, even for a short while, this servant of God, [name]. Immediately, by all that I have told you, flee from this person, as smoke flees before the wind, as wax melts before the fire. So immediately and without delay, get away in the manner and condition that I ordered before.

As, by the hand of the blessed James Zebediah, Filetus was liberated from the evil bonds of Hermogenes, so by the authority of our Lord, Jesus Christ, the crucified Nazarene, I exhort and contest and with power exorcise you, most nefarious and abominable spirits, who vex this creature of God, [name], and who continue to possess him and molest him with your obstinate rebellion. With virile force, I command you, ✝ I force you, I order you to flee and I expel you with all the power of God the Fa✝ther, by all the wisdom of God the S✝on, by all the virtue of God the Holy ✝ Spirit, for Christ conquers, ✝ Christ reigns, ✝ Christ rules. Conquered and set to fleeing by the authority of our Lord, Jesus Christ, the crucified Nazarene, I order you immediately to come out of this servant of God, [name], in the way and condition that I imposed on you before. Without delay or hesitation, go into the wilderness where you can no longer harm any other creature of God. Let this servant of God, [name], after so much molestation, regain his health, and never come back to haunt him. Otherwise, by all that I have said, with great severity, with power, and with the authority of our Lord, Jesus Christ, the crucified Nazarene, from this instant, I command and order Lucifer, Beelzebul, Satan, and all the infernal furies to immediately and ceaselessly rise against you and sink you into the pool of fire and sulfur, in the infernal abyss where you have been condemned to burn forever. With no exception, may they tie you down there with all the punishments, none excluded, and, since you are rebellious against God and his holy names, may they torment you and afflict you till the day of judgment. Amen.

EXORCISM

I drive you away, ✝ oh devil, by the worthy annunciation that the angel Gabriel made to the Virgin Mary, saying: "Hail, Mary, full of grace, the Lord is with you." And by the humble and prudent response that the Virgin gave to the angel, saying: "You see before you the Lord's servant, let it happen to me as you have said." By the reverence that John the Baptist showed toward our Lord, Jesus Christ, when both were still in the bodies of their mothers. And by the birth of the same Lord, Jesus Christ, by the swaddling clothes in which he was wrapped, by the water with which he was washed for the first time, and by the miracles that were manifested when Christ was born; by the annunciation that the angel gave to the shepherds, saying: "I bring you news of great joy: today the Savior of the world has been born to you." By the circumcision of Christ, by the offering of the Virgin Mary when she presented him in the temple, and by the reverence shown him by Simeon, when he said: "Now, oh Lord, let your servant go in peace," and for the dispute that Jesus Christ had in the temple and by his holy baptism, when John baptized him in the river Jordan; by the dove that was the figure of the Holy Spirit above his head, and by the wondrous voice of God saying: "This is my Son, the Beloved; my favor rests on him." By all of this, I order you immediately to go away from this creature of God, [name], invoking these holy names of God and Christ: Hagios, ✝ Soter, ✝ Messiah, ✝ Sabaoth, ✝ Immanuel, ✝ Adonai, ✝ ho Theòs, ✝ Athànatos, ✝ Tetragram, ✝ Jesus ✝ Christ, ✝ Elohim, ✝ Homousios, ✝ Savior, ✝ Alpha and Omega, ✝ Firstborn, ✝ Beginning and End, ✝ Way, ✝ Truth, ✝ Life, ✝ Virtue, ✝ Paraclete, ✝ Wisdom, ✝ Mediator, ✝ Lamb, ✝ Sheep, ✝ Lion, ✝ Mouth, ✝ Word, ✝ Image, ✝ Light, ✝ Glory, ✝ Sun, ✝ Splendor, ✝ Bread, ✝ Fountain, ✝ Door, ✝ Husband, ✝ Shepherd, ✝ Priest, ✝ Prophet, ✝ Saint, ✝ Almighty, ✝ Merciful, ✝ Immortal God, ✝ Peaceful King, ✝ East, ✝ Love, ✝ Mountain, ✝ Eternal, ✝ Creator, ✝ Redeemer, ✝ Vine, ✝ Star, ✝ Substance, ✝ Goodness, ✝ Supreme Good, ✝ Hope, ✝ Faith, ✝ Honor, ✝ Spirit, ✝ Ischyròs, ✝ Flower, ✝ Son, ✝ First ✝ and ✝

Last. Defend, then, Lord God, this servant of yours, [name], from the devil and from all the spirits who torment him day and night, during every hour of the day and of the night; by all your most holy names and by your mercy, grant what we ask, oh Son of the living God; have pity on us and on your servant, [name], oppressed by the devil and by the unclean spirits. You have said: "Ask and you will receive, knock and it will be opened, seek and you will find; now I too ask, knock, and seek. And as you promised in your name, so now may it come about by your infinite power, virtue, and mercy. Amen.

EXORCISM

I exorcise you, ✝ all the spirits who haunt this creature of God, [name], whatever your name and whatever the authority referred to by all those who help you. As minister of our Lord, Jesus Christ, having full authority, freedom, and power, I command you now severely, I order you and I force you to go away by these most holy names of God: El, ✝ Elohim, ✝ Adonai, ✝ Shaddai, ✝ Yah, ✝ Jehovah, ✝ Agla, ✝ Immanuel, ✝ Hagios, ✝ ho Theòs, ✝ Ischyròs, ✝ Athànatos, ✝ Alpha and ✝ Omega; holy, holy, holy, the Lord God Sabaoth, Father, Word, and Holy Spirit, most holy Trinity, only God, creator of all things. Immediately and without delay, having removed all obstacles, oh spirits who haunt this image of God and torment it by inhabiting it, come out from every hiding place and come up to the surface of the tongue; do not move without my permission and tell me the truth about everything I shall ask. Speak clearly and openly, so that I can understand well. I command you, then, by all that which in the name of Jesus Christ can force, bind, and afflict you, to tell me now why you have come upon this creature of God, [name], why you are haunting him; always obey all of my commands. Otherwise, by all I have said before, oh all you spirits who have invaded this creature of God, [name], I cast you into the depths of the abyss and, with power, I bind you in such a way that you cannot be unbound till the last day of judgment, with no exception and by authority of our Lord, Jesus Christ, the crucified Nazarene, who said: "These will be the signs that accompany those who believe in me. In my name, they will chase out devils, they will speak new tongues, they will take serpents into their hands and, if they drink poison, it will not harm them; they will lay their hands on the sick and these will be healed."

And as the very Word that was God was made flesh, and was born as a man from the Virgin Mary, and lived on the Earth, true God and true man, a single person, who preached the good news of eternal salvation, who healed the sick, forgave sins and resurrected the dead, so I, a minister of God the Father, ✝ the Son, ✝ and the Holy ✝ Spirit, exhort you, drive you away, force you and virily oblige you: all of you, with the greatest severity, I command and order to obey me in everything, with no delay and in truth, now and forever. Amen.

Here, the exorcist asks about everything concerning the expulsion of the devil and the liberation of the possessed person. Then he continues thus:

EXORCISM

I exorcise you, ✝ oh devil, by him whose birth was announced by the angel to the Virgin Mary; by he who descended from heaven for us sinners, was made flesh by the work of the Holy Spirit, was born of the Virgin Mary, and was made a man. I exorcise you, ✝ oh, devil, by that same Jesus Christ who wanted to lie in the manger dressed in humble swaddling clothes, who, needful of everything, like a child, was nourished with the milk of the Virgin; who was announced to the shepherds; who wanted to be

circumcised to fulfill the law. I exorcise you, oh devil, by
that same Lord who was manifested to the Magi, guided
by the star; who was presented in the temple and taken
into the arms of the elderly Simeon, and then fled to
Egypt.

I exorcise you, ✝ oh devil, by he who was found in
the temple amidst the doctors, who wanted to be baptized by John, who fasted in the desert for forty days and
forty nights and wanted to be tempted by the devil. I
exorcise you, ✝ oh devil, by that same Jesus who was
invited to the wedding and changed the water into wine;
who gave sight to the blind, made the deaf hear, the lame
walk; and who, with his power and virtue, healed the
sick. I exorcise you, ✝ oh devil, by means of he who
drove devils out of the bodies of the possessed, cleaned
the lepers, gave back sight to the man born blind, and
walked on the waters with dry feet. I exorcise you, ✝ oh
devil, by the same Lord who, on Mount Tabor, was trans-
figured before the disciples, who answered the prayers of
the woman from Cana, who invoked him for the sake of
her daughter, who did not despise the tears of the woman
caught in adultery.

I exorcise you, ✝ oh devil, for he who wanted to be
called a drinker and demoniac; who withstood poverty
and indigence; who wept with Mary and Martha at the
tomb of the dead Lazarus; who, after four days, raised
from the tomb that same Lazarus, in spite of the stink of
death; who, foreseeing the desolation of Jerusalem, wept
over the city. I exorcise you, ✝ oh devil, by that same
Jesus who deigned to wash the feet of his disciples; who,
at the Last Supper, with his most holy words, changed the
bread and wine into his body and blood; and, as the time
for his passion grew near, prayed to the Father till he
sweated blood, and wanted to be betrayed by a kiss from
his disciple Judas. I exorcise you, ✝ oh devil, by that same
Lord who was derided by the impious, bound in chains,

and led to the high priests; he was accused at the Sanhedrin and let himself be struck in the face with blows and slaps.

I exorcise you, ✝ oh devil, by that same Jesus who was covered with spitting and insults, who let his face be veiled, was struck by hand and fist, was struck with calumny and various insults, and wanted to be tied naked to the column and whipped till he bled for our sakes. I exorcise you, ✝ oh devil, by that same Lord, justly called "King of the Jews," who was unjustly judged by Pilate, by his command was whipped, was dressed again in a scarlet mantle and, burdened with the wood of the cross, was placed between two thieves. I exorcise you, ✝ oh devil, by he who, in front of everyone was stripped of his clothing and, stretching out his arms, was nailed to the cross, and was then insulted by the passersby and by the high priests themselves.

I exorcise you, ✝ oh devil, by he whose lips, full of sweetness and kindness, were burnt by thirst; who showed his fine face deformed like a leper's because of the blows he had received, and who prayed to the Father for those who crucified him; on the cross, he answered the prayer of the good thief and entrusted his Mother to his disciple John. I exorcise you, oh devil, by he who, in his thirst, was given bile and vinegar to drink and who, shouting out loud to his Father, said, "Into your hands I give my spirit"; then, bending his holy head, he died. I exorcise you, ✝ oh devil, by he who, with his precious blood, has redeemed the world; who had his side rent with a spear, and blood and water came. I exorcise you, ✝ oh devil, by he who was taken down from the cross in the evening and was buried in a new tomb; going down to hell with great power, he broke the bronze doors and, with his force, defeated the devil, and triumphed over hell. I exorcise you, ✝ oh devil, by he who, rising from the dead on the third day, appeared to Mary Magdalene and the disciples; over them, he sent the Holy Spirit and, after forty days, before their eyes he ascended into heaven. After fifty days, he sent down upon them the Holy Spirit paraclete with tongues of fire. By that same Lord who will come to judge with fire the living and the dead, and you as well, oh accursed evil, together with the entire world, I order you to come out immediately and to go away from this servant of God, [name], with all your iniquities, spells, curses, bonds, and evil auguries, never to return to him again. Do not forget, accursed Satan, do not forget, condemned creature, reprobate and damned by God eternally for your iniquity; do not forget, unclean spirit, wherever you hide in the body of this creature of God, [name], do not forget that the day of eternal judgment is imminent for you, the day will come like a burning oven, in which, for you and all your apostate angels, the moment of eternal perdition will come. Therefore, spirit who is condemned and to be condemned for your iniquity, honor the living, true God ✝; honor Jesus ✝ Christ, our Savior; honor the Holy ✝ Spirit paraclete in whose name and by whose power I command you, unclean spirit, wherever you hide in the body of this man [name], to go out and get away from him, never more to return, for our Lord and God, Jesus Christ, has deigned to call this man to his holy grace and blessing; he made him go to the baptismal font as a gift of his kindness, so that he would become his temple in the remission of all sins. This I command you, by the name and power of the same God and Lord, Jesus Christ, who will come to judge with fire the living and the dead of the entire world. Amen.

EXORCISM

May our Lord, Jesus Christ, the Son of God, pursue you; then, may the angels of God pursue you; may the archangels, patriarchs, and prophets pursue you; may the apostles and evangelists pursue you; may the martyrs and confessors, the virgins and all the saints and the chosen of God pursue you.

May all your arts and snares disappear, then, at all hours of the day. Surrender your force, oh rebels against God; give back health to the soul, do not tempt it or give it over to death; do not creep into food, or drink, or homes; do not attack this person when he is awake or when he sleeps, do not harm him, do not suffocate his voice, and do not prevent him from seeking eternal life.

Here, the exorcist makes a cross on all the body parts of the afflicted person, saying:

> Get away, then, in the name of the eternal God, from the head, from the hair, from the top of the head, from the forehead, from the eyes, from the tongue, from underneath the tongue, from the ears, from the nostrils, from the neck, from the jaws, from the teeth, from the throat, from the gums, from the mouth, from the palate, from the brain, from the folds of the brain, from the eyelashes and from the eyebrows, from the hairs, from the feet, from the tibias, from the knees, from the legs, from the intimate parts, from the back and sides, from the upper and lower intestines, from the femur, from the belly, from the stomach, from the heart, from the shoulders and from the back, from the chest, from the breast, from the arms, from the hands, from the fingernails, from the bones, from the nerves, from the veins, from the bone marrow, from the lungs, from the structure of the body parts, from each joint, from all the body, from all the parts of the body, from the outer and inner garments, from all the flesh, from all the skin, everywhere you hide or can hide: detach yourselves from this creature of God, [name], as the Lord God separated heaven from Earth, light from the darkness, truth from lies,

good from evil; thus, oh most unclean spirits, be separated from this creature of God, [name], now and forever. I order this of you, by he who will come to judge with fire the living and the dead and the entire world. Amen.

Sixth Exorcism
MIGHTY, TERRIBLE, AND OF MARVELOUS EFFICACY FOR DRIVING OUT UNCLEAN SPIRITS FROM POSSESSED BODIES, AND WHOSE PRACTICE PROPERLY BELONGS TO PRIESTS

The exorcist who prepares to combat demons, after observing the rules established in the first exorcism, kneels and devotedly recites Psalm 51.

ANTIPHONY

Do not remember, Lord, our crimes or those of our parents; do not take revenge for our sins.

> *Kyrie eleison. Christe eleison. Kyrie eleison.*
> Our Father. . . (*all recite the Lord's Prayer*)
> And lead us not into temptation.

> BUT DELIVER US FROM EVIL.

> Lord, hear my prayer.

> AND MAY MY CRY REACH YOU.

> The Lord be with you.

> AND WITH YOUR SPIRIT.

PRAYER

Oh most high Creator, who created all things from nothing, and dividing heaven from Earth, put a limit even to the sea, so that no one can cross it; you who formed creatures with various elements and chose to give each being its own virtue; a sinner, marked by your name and regenerated in the waters of baptism, I supplicate you to show mercy, so that, as you gave your holy apostles power over the evil spirits and the force to drive them out of human bodies, so in your holy mercy and by the gift of your grace, may it be granted to me, your unworthy servant [name], to have the power to drive out evil spirits from this creature, [name], in virtue and by invocation of your most holy name. By Christ, our Lord. Amen.

PRAYER

Oh supreme majesty, ineffable essence, most high wisdom of God, Alpha and Omega, without beginning or end, Word without time, to whom all things are possible. Oh ineffable and marvelous divinity, highest power, most-high energy, oh creator of heaven and Earth, who sits on your supreme throne and observes the immensity of the heavens and the depths of the abyss. All things that exist are before you: enlighten, then, now, and forever, and heal with the gift of your grace and salvation this creature of yours, [name], whom you have formed in your image, and break all the bonds of the evil spirits who keep him tied each day; make him free of every infestation and molestation with which they torment him.

As you liberated David from the evil sword and Jonah from the belly of the whale, Daniel from the lions' den and the three youths from the burning furnace, and Peter from the hand of Herod and from everything awaiting the Jews, so, Lord, Jesus Christ, together with the Father and the

Holy Spirit, by your immense goodness and by the prayers of your mother the Virgin Mary, and of all your saints, deign to free from every torment of evil spirits this creature of yours, [name], who was redeemed by your blood and regenerated in the waters of baptism; invoking your holy power, free him and give him, now and forever, a perfect faith in his liberation and your fear and love, so that he will serve you always and renounce Satan and all the evil spirits. By your holy medicine, let him return to the health he enjoyed before. We ask you this, through Jesus Christ, who lives and reigns in the perfect Trinity forever and ever. Amen.

PRAYER

Lord, holy God, almighty Father, you who are Alpha and Omega, that is beginning and end, without origin and termination that living man knows, most-high king and sovereign emperor, you who are God, king of kings, and lord of rulers; but also pious, merciful, clement, benign, glorious, and wondrous in your saints, you who hold the world in your hands and, with your power, keep alive everything that has been created; you who enclose the firmament of the heavens, who observe the abysses and the celestial thrones, who sustain the mountains and hold the Earth in the palm of your hands; you have made the angelic spirits as your ministers, similar to fire's flame; you make the winds come out of their abode, you struck the firstborn of Egypt, from men to animals; you divided the light from darkness, and set the great lights of the Sun and Moon in the sky. Oh God of all mercy, I as well, [name], your creature, was redeemed by the blood of your Son and regenerated in the waters of baptism. I am your servant, though I am an unworthy and miserable sinner. In the indigence of my frailty and through lack of force, I come to you with trust as to a safe haven and special refuge; I pray, my God and Lord, with reverence and love, and I humbly supplicate, as I know and am able, that you will deign to accept me now in your holy service and in the exercise of this exorcist's art, with all the power of your words; do not punish me according to what my sins deserve, for their weight burdens me and my imprudence drags me after them. You who are clement, pious, merciful, propitious, and benign, assist me and have pity on me, a poor sinner.

Have pity on me, Lord, for your mercy is greater than all the sins and crimes I have committed from the day and hour of my birth to the present day and hour; your mercy is so great that I cannot express it; for this reason, deign to answer my prayers now and always, as you deigned to answer the three youths in the burning furnace, as you answered the prophet Jonah in the belly of the whale and the apostle Peter when he was chained in prison. Listen to me as you listened to Mary Magdalene, who invoked forgiveness for her sins, and as you deigned to listen to the publican in the temple. Listen to me, as you listened to the prayers of your Mother at the wedding at Cana, as you listened to the thief on the cross and to Saint Catherine at the torture of the wheel. Most sweet Father, deign to answer my prayer; show now your power and mercy, which I implore of you with trust; by your goodness, grant me, a sinner, your unworthy servant, the gift of grace that I ask of you with all my heart, for you said: "Ask and you shall receive"; and also: "He who comes to me will not be driven away." Therefore now, I pray that, by your power and by the gift of your grace, I, a sinner and your unworthy servant, may be granted the force and energy to drive out all the nefarious spirits that are in this creature of yours, [name]; make them come out from everywhere, from the outer and inner places, when they hear your holy name and these holy words; make me able to expel them without opposition or rebellion, so as to relegate them to the depths of the abyss, without them ever being able to return again.

Make them come out with a clear sign, without harming this body and without injuring any Christian; on the contrary, let them come out and give back to this creature his earlier health.

May this gift of your grace be granted me through you, oh good Jesus, who, together with the Father and the Holy Spirit, are the only true God and creator. And so as not to fall into the vice of ingratitude, I praise you, I adore you, I bless you, and I glorify you; now and perpetually, I shall serve you with all my devotion, forever and ever. Amen.

Here, the exorcist rises from prayer and reads the following passage from the gospels:

From the Gospel according to Luke (9:1–6):

He called the Twelve together and gave them power and authority over all devils and to cure diseases, and he sent them out to proclaim the kingdom of God and to heal. He said to them, "Take nothing for the journey: neither staff, nor haversack, nor bread, nor money; and do not have a spare tunic. Whatever house you enter, stay there; and when you leave, let your departure be from there. As for those who do not welcome you, when you leave their town, shake the dust from your feet as evidence against them." So they set out and went from village to village proclaiming the good news and healing everywhere.

PRAISE TO YOU, OH CHRIST.

PRAYER

Almighty and eternal God, who in the beginning created from the void the heavens, the Earth, and the sea, and all things held in them; you who love everything you have formed, and seek out virtue and scatter vices, so deign to set fleeing this evil spirit who pursues this creature of yours, [name]. He truly believes in you and in your Son, our liberator and Lord, Jesus Christ, and he believes in the Holy Spirit that proceeds from the Father and from the Son. I as well, in his name, believe in you, in your Son, the true liberator and Lord, Jesus Christ, and in the Holy Spirit that proceeds from the Father and the Son. Amen.

Here, the exorcist shall say the following exorcism in a loud voice, with a strong spirit and great courage, inveighing against the spirit living within the obsessed person.

EXORCISM

Listen with your intellect, oh unclean spirit: I exorcise you by God the Fa✝ther almighty, by God the S✝on, and by God the Holy ✝ Spirit. I admonish you and command you, nefarious spirit, who are and abide in this body or around it: by God almighty, creator of heaven and Earth, and by that power that cast you down from heaven because of your pride, by the force and in virtue of the holy names of god, I order you to obey immediately and with ready effect, without resistance or rebellion, the divine words, the holy names, all the formulas proffered by me and each one of my commands. May God arise and may his enemies be scattered; may those who hate him flee from his face. As smoke disappears, so may you disappear as well, evil spirit, who inhabits this creature of God, [name], or around it; gets away, disgraceful spirit, from this servant of God, [name], and he will see the justice of his Lord. May fear and trembling come upon you for the greatness and power of the name of God. May your ways be dark and slippery, and may the angels of God pursue you, that is Michael, Gabriel, Raphael, and all the other angelic spirits; may they chase you away, accursed spirit, from this servant of God, [name], so that you can no longer return to him: may this again be prohibited to you and all unclean spirits. In the name of the Fa✝ther, of the S✝on, and of the Holy ✝ Spirit. Amen.

May God the Father command you, may God the Son force you, may God the Holy Spirit and all the Trinity together command you, oh devil who lives inside or around this creature of God, [name]. And I command you as well, miserable spirit, by these glorious names of God: Alpha and Omega, Agla, Shaddai, Adonai, Hagios, ho Theòs, Ischyròs, Athànatos, Sabaoth, God, non-created Father, Son, and Holy Spirit; immediately and without harming any living creature, get away from this servant of God, [name], and leave him healthy as you found him; accursed devil, leave him without delay and never return again, you or others.

Christ reigns, ✝ Christ wins, ✝ Christ orders ✝ you, unclean spirit, who lives in the body of this man, and I order you as well, evil devil, by the most holy names of God: Tetragram, El, Immanuel, Elohim, Paraclete, God, Immense Father, Son, and Holy Spirit. Listen to my words, hurry out of this servant of God, in spite of any tie holding you back; do not harm him in any way, but leave him healthy as when you first came to him, and never again come back to him in any other way.

And by the authority of our Lord, Jesus Christ, I unbind you, [name], from this unclean spirit, and may all the bonds and ties of any condition, power, and force by which such a spirit is held in this body be broken and undone. May this be achieved by virtue of our Lord, Jesus Christ. Amen.

Therefore, may any way of return be forbidden you, oh accursed spirit, by the works of God, the almighty Father, and of my Lord, Jesus Christ; thus also may the way be barred to all the evil spirits of any kind, power, and force. By the same, ✝ with the same, ✝ and in the same ✝ God, by these venerable names: Athànatos, Soter, God, Eternal Father and Son and Holy Spirit; by the authority of our Lord, Jesus Christ, by all the words I have pronounced and that I shall say, most vile spirit, rebellious, evil, nefarious, unclean and filthy, accursed by God and by the most pure Virgin Mary, by all the holy angels and archangels, by the thrones, dominions, principalities, and celestial powers, by the cherubim and seraphim, by the patriarchs and prophets, by the martyrs, by the confessors, by the virgins and by all the saints, as well as by the glorious hosts of heaven, I order you to be bound up, immersed, and tied in the deepest place of hell, where you will be cruelly tortured by all the demons now and eternally, by divine commandment. Amen.

And may the curse of God, the almighty Father, of the Son, and of the Holy Spirit, the wrath and indignation of all the angels, the saints of God, and all the heavenly court, as well as all the creatures, descend immediately and without delay and with supreme furor over Lucifer, Beelzebul, Satan, and over all the princes of the devils. May no one any longer obey these evil spirits, or fear or venerate them, but may the devils immediately rise up against them by virtue of all the names of almighty God. If again, oh evil spirit, they come to assist you, may all your power and force be broken in the name of the great and almighty God, so that you can no longer inhabit this body, and may no one give you help, but may all the spirits, everywhere they are found, be against you, accursed spirit, rebellious against the divine names and words. May the great angels of God, Saint Michael, Saint Gabriel, and Saint Raphael, and all those named before who are powerful in battle, come down. As by divine command they made all the spirits rebellious to God fall down from heaven, and sent them from their glorious abodes into the deepest abyss, so with equal force, may they immediately cast you out of this creature of God, [name], doing him no harm, without injuring or frightening any Christian. May they hold you bowed down with their power in the deepest place in hell, from which you will never again emerge. The head of all the devils is plotting against you and will torment you eternally a hundred times more cruelly than usual, by means of he who established the day of judgment and by all his holy works, his heavenly hosts, and his holy names. Amen.

EXORCISM OF THE AIR

I exorcise you, ✝ air, by God, the almighty Father, by his only Son, our Lord, and by the Holy Spirit paraclete; by the Virgin Mary, mother of our Lord, Jesus Christ, undefiled and uncorrupted; by him whom you obeyed when you commanded the winds and the sea and immediately a great calm descended; by the angels, the archangels, the thrones, dominions, principalities, and powers, the heavenly hosts, the cherubim and seraphim who flew for you, when Christ was born, singing: "Glory to God in the highest, and peace on Earth to men of good will." And by all the saints of God, by all the heavenly court; by all the merits and prayers of all the saints of God and of the heavenly court, who each day give honor to Jesus Christ, our Lord, Son of God, born of the Virgin Mary: may you, air, no longer have the capacity to contain this accursed, evil, and nefarious spirit, nor any of those who favor it; but drive it away from you, together with its assistants, as the blessed Virgin Mary rejected every stain of sin. Amen.

Again I exorcise you, ✝ oh air, and all the beings that in you and of you live and in you remain, by God, the almighty Father, creator of heaven and Earth, by Holy Mary, mother of our Lord, Jesus Christ. And by Saint John Baptist, by all the angels and archangels, the thrones, dominions, principalities, and powers, the hosts of cherubim and seraphim; by all the patriarchs and prophets, by all the apostles and evangelists of God, by all the disciples of our Lord, Jesus Christ, by all the holy martyrs, the pontifices, confessors, and doctors of God, the monks and hermits; by all the holy priests, levites, and by all the holy virgins of God, by all the celestial court and the holy prayers and supplications that each day are made there; by the holy sacrifice of the Mass, which each day is celebrated all over the world in honor of our Lord, Jesus Christ, and by all those invocations with which, in the name of Jesus Christ, the devils can be exorcised and forced to obey, I command you, oh air, not to contain any longer this evil spirit nor those who help it. I command you this in the name of he who will come to judge with fire the living and the dead and the entire world. Amen.

EXORCISM OF THE EARTH

I exorcise you, ✝ oh Earth, by god One-in-Three, by Jesus Christ, our Lord, who was conceived by the work of the Holy Spirit, was born from the Virgin Mary, was made man, and for our sakes was crucified; in you, he was buried. You knew him and, recognizing him, you trembled. I exorcise you by the glorious tomb of Christ, which was dug in you, and by all the celestial court of the most-high, great, and tremendous God; by all the prayers and supplications raised each day therein. I command you not to hold this evil spirit in any way, or those who favor it, but immediately and without delay, despite any bond holding it back in this body, make it go away without causing harm or molestation to this creature of God, [name], or to other Christians. Oh Earth, absorb immediately and with haste this devil, rebellious to God, as you absorbed Dathan and Abiram, by the power of almighty God, your creator, who deigned to inhabit you in human form. As the fish threw up Jonah from its belly and did not hold him back, thus may you not be able to hold back this evil spirit or those who favor it, whatever their condition and strength, but make it remain forever in the most wretched place in lower hell, together with all its helpers. Amen.

Oh Earth, as the sea monster swallowed up the prophet Jonah, but could not hold him, thus you, by the name,

force, and authority of our Lord, Jesus Christ, the crucified
Nazarene, by the sign of the holy cross, ✝ may you be
unable to hold this evil spirit, but swallow it up and absorb
it immediately, after hearing my words. Make it be cast by
a powerful hand into lower hell, where it will be tortured
with eternal torments a hundred-fold more cruel than
usual, without ever being able to get out till the day of the
last judgment. Amen.

Again I exorcise all things that are found in you and lie
in you and live off you, oh Earth, by Jesus Christ, our Lord,
the Son of God, and by the glorious virgin, his Mother; by
Saint John Baptist, by all the holy angels, archangels,
thrones and dominions, principalities, powers, hosts of
cherubim and seraphim; and by all the holy patriarchs and
prophets; by all the holy apostles and evangelists of God; by
all the disciples of our Lord, Jesus Christ, by the martyrs,
the pontifices, confessors, doctors, monks, and hermits of
God. By all the holy priests and levites of God, by the holy
virgins, the widows and persons who live in chastity; by all
the heavenly court and all the holy prayers and supplications that are raised to you every day therein; by the holy
sacrifice of the Mass, which each day is celebrated in the
orb of the universe in honor of our Lord, Jesus Christ; and
by the tombs and bodies of all the saints of God who are
placed in you; and by the footprints of Christ and of all the
saints of God, I order you to let this evil spirit depart along
with all those who favor it. May it be led to lower hell, and
may you not in any way hold it, nor may it be able to
remain with you or inside you, but may it flee like dust
before the wind, together with all its helpers. Amen.

EXORCISM OF WATER

I exorcise you, ✝ oh water, wherever you are, large or
small, by Jesus Christ, Son of God, by whose feet you let
yourself be trampled and whose words you have always

obeyed; by the staff of Moses, at whose stroke you withdrew before the people of God; by the water that came out of the side stricken by Longinus; by the holy baptism that is performed with you; by holy Mary, mother of our Lord, Jesus Christ, and by all the angels and archangels, by the patriarchs, the prophets, the apostles, the evangelists, and by all the holy Innocents, the martyrs, confessors, doctors, and hermits of God; by all the celestial court and by all the prayers and supplications performed therein to the Lord God, I order you not to be able to hold this evil spirit or those who favor it, but may it and all its companions be expelled in haste from you, with great furor and impetus, as Christ drove out the seven devils from the body of Mary Magdalene, so that it will be carried to the deepest place in hell, to remain there forever, tormented more cruelly than usual. Amen.

EXORCISM OF FIRE

I exorcise you, ✝ oh fire, wherever you are or burn, by the Lord God, Father almighty, who appeared to Moses in the form of fire; by he who freed the three youths from the burning furnace and by all the saints given in burnt offerings who were made with fire, in praise of God almighty; by all the angels and saints of God, I order you no longer to be able in any way to hold this spirit or those who favor it, but let them be carried immediately and without delay, at the sound of my word, to lower hell, where they shall burn in the fire of the immense, hard flame, and in no way may they be able to come out of it till the day of judgment, and may they be tormented forever with punishments more cruel than usual. Amen.

Again I exorcise ✝ everything that is found in you and remains in you and lives off you, by the Lord God, Father almighty, who appeared to Moses in the form of fire; by he who freed the three youths from the furnace of burning fire;

by holy Mary, mother of our Lord, Jesus Christ, by Saint John Baptist, by all the holy angels and archangels, thrones and dominions, principalities, powers, hosts of cherubim and seraphim. By the holy patriarchs and prophets, by the apostles and the evangelists of God, by all the holy disciples of our Lord, Jesus Christ; by the holy martyrs, confessors, and doctors, by all the holy priests and levites, by the monks and holy hermits of God, by the virgins, widows, and those who live in chastity; by all the heavenly court and all the holy prayers and supplications performed therein each day; by the holy sacrifice of the Mass, which each day is celebrated on the universe-Earth in honor of our Lord, Jesus Christ, and by everything that in the name of Jesus Christ can be used to exorcise and force the devils to obedience, I order you, oh fire, not to hold any longer this evil spirit, rebellious to God, or those who help it. I command you this by he who will come to judge with fire the living and the dead and the entire world. Amen.

EXORCISM OF ALL THE ELEMENTS

I exorcise ✝ all things composed of the four elements, all things that live off them or are found in, inhabit, and remain in them, in any place and part of the world they may be; by the force and almighty power of God, the great and almighty, of his Son, and of the Holy Spirit; by the holy fast and the holy life that Christ led in the desert; by the abstinence, the prayers, and all the good works done by all the saints of God; by all the holy angels of God, and by everything that, in the name of Jesus, can force and oblige the devils, I order you immediately to expel this evil spirit, as soon as you have heard my words. May it be led by a powerful hand into lower hell, there to be tormented in a crueler way than usual, and may it remain there forever, with all those who help it, till the day of judgment, never to emerge. Amen.

EXORCISM OF HELL

Oh hell, infernal fire and all you punishments of the depths, infernal princes and devils, heed, hear, and understand the words of my mouth. I exorcise ✝ you by he who, after four days, brought back Lazarus from the stink of death to life; before him you trembled, full of fear, and with you all your servants were dismayed, oh hell, and you could not hold back Lazarus.

Oh hell, infernal fire, and all your punishments of the depths with all its devils, I command you with power in the name of he who subjected you to his dominion; by his power and might, listen to my words: I order you to obey us by the authority of our Lord, Jesus Christ, fulfilling all our orders according to his will. It is the holy Trinity, Father, Son, and Holy Spirit, that commands you, oh hell, to obey me immediately. The battalions of the angels command this of you. The choir of patriarchs commands it of you, the hosts of the prophets command it of you, so that, having heard and understood my order, you will comply immediately and concretely. I exorcise you ✝ oh hell, infernal fire, and your punishments of the depths with all its devils, of any sort and category, by he who broke open your doors and knocked down your barriers; who tore the holy fathers away from you and in you relegated the evil devils, commanding that they should be tormented forever in your bowels. With the powerful arm of his divinity, it was he who chained up the violence of the devils.

I also exorcise you by Mary, the holy Mother of our Lord, Jesus Christ, by Saint John Baptist, by all the holy angels and archangels, by the thrones, dominions, princi-palities, and powers, the hosts of cherubim and seraphim, by all the holy patriarchs and prophets, by the apostles and the evangelists, and by all the holy disciples of Christ. By the holy Innocents, the martyrs, confessors, and doctors of God, by all the holy priests and levites, by the monks and

hermits, by all the holy virgins, widows, and persons living
in chastity; by the tremendous day of judgment, by the
almighty power of all the celestial court, and by all the
words with which it is possible to exorcise, bind, and force
you, hell and infernal fire with all your devils; by all this, in
the name of Jesus Christ, I exorcise you, oh Lucifer, Prince
of Hell, so that you will not permit this evil spirit to remain
anywhere, but will drag it with you, and make it come
away in haste, with all your fury and indignation; carry
away even those who help it, despite bonds of any kind that
keep it in this body. May all ties be broken and reduced to
nothing, and may they disappear like smoke dissolving. All
of you devils, of whatever condition and state, and your
punishments of infernal fire, and you, hell, by everything
that I have said till now, immediately break out against this
evil spirit and its helpers; strike it hard with punishments a
thousand times more cruel than usual. Oh hell, immediately
send your powers and your mighty punishments against
this spirit, rebellious against God, call it immediately to
you, for he who broke down your doors orders this of you.
Amen.

EXORCISM

I exorcise you, ✝ evil spirits and infernal and Earthly devils, who are in fire, in the air, and in the water, and all you
evil spirits, wherever you are or wherever you abide. May
all my exorcisms come against you with force and supreme
power; may my words surround you and afflict you greatly,
and force you by the almighty power of God to do my will,
in honor, praise, and glory of the same almighty God. By
the holy names of Jesus Christ, our Lord, by the Tetragram,
Adonai, Sabaoth, Elohim, Eloah, Messiah, Sotèr, Immanuel,
Hagios, Ischyròs, ho Theòs, Athànatos, Holy, Immortal,
Agla, Jesus Christ, Alpha and Omega, Image, Light, Glory,
Holy, Omnipotent, Merciful, God; by all these holy names,

I order you to drag away with you this evil spirit and force it to go to the deepest place of hell, together with those who help it; and may there no longer be anyone who will obey it, by the tremendous day of judgment, by he who will come to judge with fire the living and the dead of the entire world.

And as Christ was bound with chains when he was made prisoner for the sake of us sinners, was whipped, crowned with thorns, and crucified, so you, nefarious spirit, must be whipped, tortured, and cruelly struck with all the punishments of hell; and as the veil of the temple was torn in two from top to bottom, and the rocks cracked, the tombs opened up and many bodies of the saints who were dead rose; and as the Earth shook and was in upheaval, so you, nefarious spirit, must tremble and flee from this body, shaped by God; go away in haste and never again return to this servant of God, [name]. And you also, spirits who help it, tremble and flee from this creature of God, [name]. After hearing all my words, oh accursed spirit, may you no more be able to arouse fear or fright or dread, or bring any harm to me or any other creature of God, present or living, nor to any living man or creature of God who has the spirit of life; but again, go away, despite the ties that hold you to this body; and if any other obeys you or helps you, even if they are many, may the curse of God fall down upon them, of God the Father almighty, of the Son, and of the Holy Spirit; may the wrath and indignation of the holy Trinity, of all the angels, and of the entire celestial court fall down upon you; and may there be no one who dares to obey this spirit, rebellious to God, for I command this of you by the Son of the supreme God. Amen.

Here, the exorcist must interrogate the possessed person, as said in the other exorcisms. Then he continues in this manner:

EXORCISM

I exorcise you ✝ with force and power, all you evil spirits, large and small, wherever you are, wherever you make your home; and I order you with authority, I command you severely and I order you by my Lord God almighty, whom you fear and cannot see; by Jesus Christ, Son of God, and by the Holy Spirit paraclete; by the Virgin Mary, mother of our Lord, Jesus Christ, undefiled and uncorrupted, your scourge and my help, by her most precious and unharmed body, by her most pure virginity, and by all the precious parts of her body with which she bore our Lord, Jesus Christ, in her womb, by her perfect soul filled with all virtues, by the great power that she has over you, and by the most precious milk with which she nursed our Lord, Jesus Christ, the Son of God; and by all the angels, archangels, and the orders of the blessed spirits; by the apostles and the evangelists; by Saint John Baptist, by all the holy patriarchs, the prophets, martyrs, confessors, virgins, and widows; by all the great names of my almighty God and by those of the mother of his Son, our Lord, Jesus Christ.

And by the power and virtue of all the exorcisms, bonds, ties, and commands of any type and degree, with which, in the name of Jesus Christ, you can be driven out, forced to obey, tied up, set fleeing, tormented, afflicted, or condemned to any punishment, I order you to capture and immediately to drag away with you this evil spirit, principle of all evils, who has invaded and each day torments this creature of God, [name], trying to make him deviate from the commandments of my God; I order you not to harm and not to injure any creature, particularly this creature of God, [name], or any of those surrounding us; immediately take away this evil spirit and all those who help it or hide, whether present or absent, to the harshest place of hell, under the rule of Lucifer; tie down there with tight and powerful bonds, all the spirits who try to torment this person, make them undergo all the harshest punishments of hell by all that I have said, and all that can be said by authority of our Lord, Jesus Christ; let this evil spirit no longer emerge from hell, nor any of those who help it, until my almighty God commands you to make them emerge. If you do not immediately do what I have told you and shall tell you, may the wrath of God be against you, demons, against this evil spirit and all those who help it, and may you be tormented with all the pains and punishments of hell, remaining there forever confined, prisoners by the authority of our Lord, Jesus Christ, the crucified Nazarene, and of all the heavenly court. Amen.

EXORCISM OF FIRE

IN WHICH TO BURN THE IMAGE OF THE DEVIL PAINTED ON PAPER

Here, the exorcist must have ready a painted image of the devil oppressing the possessed person, with the name of the devil written over its head, and must exorcise the fire prepared for this purpose with the following exorcism.

EXORCISM

I exorcise you, ✝ oh fire, by God the almighty Father, who appeared to Moses in the form of fire; by he who liberated the three youths from the furnace of burning fire and by all the saints burnt as offerings, who in you and by you were made in praise of the great and almighty God, our creator; by him whose seat is fire, whose domicile is fire: he himself is fire, around him there is fire, before him inhabits fire, from his side issues the flame of fire, he who created every fire and from whom will come out a devouring flame that will precede him and strike and destroy all those who are against him and do not obey his words, not putting his will into practice.

I exorcise you, ✝ oh fire, by holy Mary, the glorious mother of our Lord, Jesus Christ, by Saint John Baptist; by all the holy angels and archangels, by the thrones, dominions, principalities and powers, the hosts of cherubim and seraphim; by the patriarchs and prophets, by all the apostles, the evangelists, and all the holy disciples of Jesus Christ; by the holy Innocents, the martyrs, confessors, virgins, and widows, by all the saints of God; by all the heavenly court, by the names of God, Agla, Tetragram, YHWH; by the name of Jesus and by the name of God who rules with power over all fire.

Again I exorcise you , ✝ oh fire, by he who makes the Earth tremble, so that immediately, with the greatest furor, after being exorcised by means of so many and such holy names of your Creator, you will burn this sheet of paper on which the devil's image is painted, the image now corresponding to the figure and name of this most disgraceful spirit; the name of this devil is written on this paper as well, placed over the head of the figure; you, exorcised fire, make this image burn at once and become ash, when I throw it into you; this is what this evil spirit well deserves, and you must burn it in a terrible way. As you will then burn and inflame this image having the name of the devil, and as, from day to day, a thousand times, you will burn and inflame this image, so must the spirit who improperly is found in the body of this person, feel in itself and in all its substance the power of fire; it must always burn and feel the horrible torment of fire till the day of judgment, and this pain and this hurt will increase a hundred-fold from hour to hour. And no spirit, of any kind, power, or force, shall dare take away this pain; no one shall obey it nor help it, by virtue of God and of the words I have said and by their power. This evil spirit, [name], shall not in any way be able to avoid leaving this body, but shall go away conquered by this punishment, and severely forced; may it immediately go away from this creature of God, [name];

may it never again return to him, but may it go away without harming his body or bringing harm to other persons, as
I ordered before. This pain of fire shall not be removed
from it, unless it goes out first, and proceeds to the depths
of the abyss; may it not have the power to emerge from
there till the day of judgment, and may there not be anyone
who can untie it from what I have said, shall say, and shall
do, by virtue of he who will come to judge with fire the living and the dead and the entire world. Amen.

Blessing of the fire

Our help is in the name of the Lord.

HE MADE HEAVEN AND EARTH.

The Lord be with you.

AND WITH YOUR SPIRIT.

PRAYER

Lord God almighty, bless ✝ this creature of fire with your
heavenly blessing, so that it can set fleeing and smoke out
the spirit who lives around or inside this image of yours,
and all those that help it; may this fire reject and send away
the aforesaid spirit from this creature of yours, [name], and
send it, together with all its assistants, to the place where
fire is never extinguished, without harming this creature
and all the others present.

You, oh Lord, who can do all things, in sanctifying this
fire, sanctify it, and in blessing, bless it, and may the punishment foreseen for this evil spirit become more and more
horrible from one hour to the next; great and most powerful God, set it fleeing and conquer it, whether it wishes or
not, wherever it is hidden in this creature made in your
image. May it go out of him without harming anyone, and
may it be bound to the depths of the abyss with all its assis-

tants; may neither it nor any other be able to return here, and may the pain of fire now begin to strike it cruelly in all its being, and may it feel the fire's force when I throw this painted image into the fire, so that it will burn, and thus its pain will grow and increase more and more atrociously from hour to hour and a thousand-fold. After I have placed this diabolical image in the fire so that it will burn there, and after it is burnt, may this evil spirit not be able to stand its pain, unless it goes away and does not ever return again, as I have commanded. This punishment will not be taken away from it, unless it withdraws first, together with its assistants, obeying your name, Jesus Christ Nazarene, the crucified, who will come to judge with fire the living and the dead and the entire world. Amen.

As wax melts before the fire and dust is dispersed before the wind, so may all its power and energy disappear so that it can no longer live and remain in this person created in your image, to your praise and glory, Lord, Jesus Christ, who will come to judge with fire the living and the dead and the entire world. Amen.

PRAYER

Oh glorious and most holy Adonai, by whom all things created are governed and remain in existence, show favor to my invocations. By your mercy and by the gift of your grace, let this fire become a blessed creature in your name, and always obtain full force and efficacy to act powerfully against this accursed spirit who for so long has despised and disobeyed the holy words proffered by me. Make this fire have the capacity to efficaciously achieve what I wish, through you, oh most holy Adonai. Amen.

Then he sprinkles the fire with holy water. After the blessing is over, sulfur, galbanum, asafoetida, birthwort, great St. John's wort, and herb-of-grace must be taken, each one blessed with its own formula, and then cast into the fire. Then the exorcist, holding over the fire the image of the devil painted and marked with its name, shall read the following exorcism.

Insults against the Evil Spirits

Hear, hear, hear, [name], spirit accursed by God, condemned eternally to perpetual punishment, nefarious, disgraced and rebellious to God; father of lies, traitor to all, root of all evil, origin of discord, instigator of vices, fool, senseless one, gossip, heretic, apostate, fetid, filthy, and evil being, devoid of any good and full of every evil, murderer, reprobate, son of perdition and of the eternal curse, enemy of mankind, you who tear life away and make justice deviate, origin of avarice, most vile serpent, rapacious wolf, object of derision for all the angels, you were ignorant, a fool, and, in your stupidity, you said in your heart: "There is no God"; recognize, then, your horrible sentence and your terrible punishment—bitter, harsh punishment, full of many scourges and much anguish. Since you have been rebellious to the divine words and names, in honor of such names, which are worthy of reverence, fear and obedience, I want to tell you immediately the punishment assured you, oh evil spirit, and I shall inflict it on you with horrible force, by the authority, virtue, and power of the great and almighty God who created heaven and Earth, and all things therein contained. He will come to judge with fire the living, the dead, and all the other devils, and the entire world. Amen.

Oh spirit, [name], nefarious and evil, by the authority, virtue, and great power of God and of all the heavenly court, may you be damned and cursed perpetually in eternal punishment: may you never have rest, unless immediately, upon hearing my words, you withdraw, confused and defeated, from this creature of God, [name], and

from his person, wherever you hide, in the way and in the
condition that I ordered repeatedly. By all the divine
names and by their virtue, by the words that all creatures
obey in trembling, by the God who unleashes thunder
and lightning to destroy you and your subjects, infamous
spirit, to expel you with power and cruelly strike you,
like lightning, with great impetus; through him, I curse
you with force, nefarious spirit, I anathematize you, I
deprive you of all your strength and power, I cast you
down and sink you into the greatest torment that is in
hell. By divine virtue, I relegate you with indissoluble
bonds to the pool of fire and sulfur, and I condemn you
eternally till the day of judgment to be horribly cremated,
and may you be forbidden any other place or location
outside the deepest center of the Earth, where your abode
is fixed till the day of judgment. There, you will be subject to all the single infernal punishments in the most
atrocious and harsh way of Lucifer. Let no one any longer
obey you, by these names of God, and by their power and
virtue: Adonai, Agla, Jesus, Tetragram, Sabaoth,
Messiah, Soter, Immanuel, Hagios, ho Theòs, Ischyròs,
Athànatos, and by all the other terrible and ineffable
names and mysteries of God, may the curse of almighty
God, Father, Son, and Holy Spirit, come and descend
upon you; may the wrath and indignation of the holy
Virgin Mary and of all the holy angels come: and of Saint
John Baptist, of all the heavenly court and all the creatures marked by the sign of the holy cross. May these
curses immediately descend upon you, upon Lucifer,
Beelzebul, Satan, Astaroth, Behemoth, Beherit, and all
the heads of demons, on all the devils of any kind and
condition, if they give you any help, oh evil spirit. May
there be no one who obeys you or them, by all I have said
and shall say; and again, by virtue and by the power of
all those I named before, by the name, majesty and power
of our great and almighty God, strong and terrible, and

in the name of Jesus Christ Nazarene, crucified for the sake of us miserable sinners, may all your powers be broken and bound in an indissoluble way, together with that of the other spirits who help you and who resist against the divine words and my command, or rather those of Jesus Christ, Son of the almighty God, with whose functions I am now invested, though I am a poor sinner with no merit, lacking in virtue and inadequate for the task entrusted me, because of my frailty.

And as Christ was tied to the column and cruelly whipped by the Jews, nailed to the cross, mercilessly crowned with thorns; and as the Earth trembled and the veil of the temple was torn in two from top to bottom, while the bodies of many saints who were dead arose, so may all I have said and will say, and all I am about to do, be enacted efficaciously upon you. Amen.

PRAYER

Lord, my God, king of kings and sovereign of sovereigns, in supplication, we pray you to grant what we ask with no delay and in haste, in the furor of your wrath, with the virtue and power with which you said: "Let there be light," and there was light; so we ask that all curses and all announced punishments that are to be uttered be made against this evil spirit; may no one come to its aid, oh Lord; may its name be canceled, for it preferred curses to blessings. Give us your help and force against this most disgraceful spirit. Help me, Lord, my God. Let your mercy descend upon us, Lord, for we have put our hopes in you. Not to us, Lord, not to us, but to your name give glory and by your benign mercy confirm every curse and punishment that, by your authority and power, I have inflicted and will inflict on this evil spirit. Extend your hand and cast lightning upon it; may the Earth devour it and may it return to the place from which it came. Amen.

Here, the exorcist throws the painted image into the fire and, addressing the devil that torments the possessed person, shall say:

May all your evil plots perish, then may they be resolved to your detriment and confusion, oh accursed spirit, for you will stumble and fall against the stone of God and you will undergo terrible punishment and eternal malediction, and you will be expulsed immediately from this creature of God, [name], wherever you hide. And now, evil spirit, I have placed your name and your diabolical image in the fire and I have made it burn with a horrible odor, so that the image and the name that is now proper to you will be immediately destroyed. As your name burns and your image is consumed by flames, so immediately, without delay, in your being and in your self, oh accursed spirit, may you eternally feel the burning of fire, and may you burn a thousand times more harshly than this fire consuming your paper image. May this punishment of fire increase constantly until the day of judgment, so that you will be defeated and forced to come out of this creature of God, [name], wherever you hide, in the way and conditions that I ordered before. May you be unable to resist this punishment in any other way, unless by withdrawing conquered and confused, and may no other spirit, large or small, of any kind or power, be so presumptuous as to take you out or resist this punishment, nor may another be able to obey you and give you any help, but instead, may what I have said immediately have effect by the power and majesty of my mighty and terrible Lord.

And you, Lord, my God, confirm my words with your power and force, now and eternally; as you confirmed, in grace, all the angels who remained with you, so now confirm everything I have said, making it become reality in your name. Amen.

Rise, Lord, in your wrath, in your ire destroy it.

May this devil come out before our feet and fall to the ground: by your furor, oh God, make this spirit come out.

The Lord frees prisoners, the Lord restores sight to the blind, the Lord raises the fallen. The Lord loves the just, the Lord protects the foreigner, he sustains the orphan and the widow, but disrupts the ways of the impious. Not to us, Lord, not to us, but to your name give glory.

The right hand of the Lord has worked miracles, the right hand of the Lord has raised me. In you, Lord, I trust: I shall not be confused in eternity. All those who hope in you will be free of confusion. Come to my aid and help me, Lord, my God. Lord, hear my prayer. And may my cry reach you.

May your ears be attentive to the voice of my supplication.

Be like a watchtower against all evil spirits. Scatter them, Lord, like straw before the wind. Amen.

EXORCISM

Again, and for the last time, I exorcise you ✝ and I drive you out, ✝ oh devil, ✝ and I contest you by the name, and with the virtue and power of the divine and immaculate Lamb, who tramples upon the serpent and the basilisk, who has driven away for eternity the lion and the infernal dragon. With power and severity, I exorcise you, ✝ most vile devil, accursed forever, evil ever since antiquity, by he who created from nothing all spirits, and by virtue of Jesus Christ, the crucified Nazarene, King of the Jews. And by virtue of all the names of God, holy, ineffable, and most potent: El, † Elohim, † Adonai, † Shaddai, † Soter, † Immanuel, † Sabaoth, † Tetragram, † Alpha and Omega, † Beginning and End, † Hagios, † Ischyròs, † ho Theòs, † Athànatos, † Agla, † Jehovah, † Homousios, † Yah, † Jesus † Christ,† Messiah, † Eloah, † Eheye. † By the ineffable power of all these names together; by the virtue of God on high, supreme and almighty, creator of heaven, Earth, and the entire universe, by means of whom all things are created and governed; by his ineffable and marvelous power, by his irresistible force that penetrates and dominates each fire; by the majesty of he who sits on a throne of fire, and before whom issues a flame that strikes and burns anyone who dares to contradict him and does not obey his words and does not immediately obey his commands. In virtue of the blessed and glorious Virgin Mary, and by the supreme power of God, by the greatness of all the works created by him, in force of all the words that I uttered before, of any kind and quality, that can in any way drive you out and force you to obey in the name of God, or else do what I want, or be condemned to some punishment that torments you; by all this, then, oh wretched serpent, I exorcise you and I command you to go away in confusion and defeat, without frightening the persons here present. Go away at once from this creature of God, [name], wherever you are hiding, from all his hair and from each part of his body, and from his person. Go away, accursed spirit, rapacious wolf, from all the woolen clothing and garments belonging to this person, and find no more place in him; may you be robbed of all power over him, despite any spell of any sort and force, made with words or in figures, with herbs, with a number of images, or on some sheet of paper; despite any bond, of any type or nature, and despite any cause that has made you come here, or that has sent you and holds you here, oh accursed devil, allowing you to inhabit and to remain in any way in this body formed by God; despite anything that has been done or should be done in your favor, oh devil, I order you to get away from here and to return no more to this creature of God, [name], you or any other diabolical spirit, of any type or condition. Immediately hear my words, descend to the depths of the abyss to be tormented eternally and more cruelly than usual. Go out of this person without harming his body or that of the persons present; leave this body healthy as it was when you entered it. Until the day of judgment, together with your helpers, may you be unable to emerge from hell, by authority of our Lord, Jesus Christ, by all that I have said, shall say, and am about to do to your detriment and in order to chase you out, in praise of almighty God.

And by authority of our Lord, Jesus Christ, by all the heavenly court and its power, by all the names I invoked before, I absolve this servant of God, [name], of all spells and incantations and of all evil auguries of any sort or nature that have been made against him or are made each day by the devil and by other evil spirits.

In the name of our Lord, Jesus Christ, and by virtue of all the words I have pronounced, may all your power be broken and destroyed, oh devil, as Christ broke with his death the gates of hell. May your force, oh nefarious spirit, which unworthily inhabits this body, be bound by all that I have said, as Satan was bound by the angel and as by the prayers of the apostle Peter, the spells of Simon the Magician were broken before the Roman people. By the power that cast you down from heaven, may all bonds, ties, and spells of any sort or nature be immediately and at once destroyed and annulled. And as the most blessed Virgin Mary and all the virgins of God enjoy with Christ eternal glory, so at this instant, in the name of Jesus Christ, the crucified Nazarene, by virtue of his passion, go away in all haste from this creature of God, [name], and go into the depths of the abyss, giving a clear sign of your departure, without harming this person or any person present, in the manner and condition I commanded before. May all your bonds, ties, and spells preventing your departure be broken.

Hear, evil spirit: from now on no longer dare to be or remain in this body formed by God; wherever you are hiding, whether inside or out, by virtue of all those I have invoked, I command you with force and I order you severely to go away, by the authority of our Lord, Jesus Christ. Flee, flee, flee, most vile being and rebellious against God, from his names and all the holy names I have said. Give up your place, oh pitiless one, give up your place to Jesus Christ, oh impious one: go away immediately, most vile spirit, and may no one obey you or help you. Otherwise, I shall repeat everything I have already said, in praise of God and for your confusion. I shall cast you into the pool of fire and sulfur, there to be eternally consumed; I shall condemn you to stay there till the day of judgment, I shall curse you with terrible power. I shall cast an anathema on you and I shall tie you tightly in the depths of hell, where you shall never have repose, for all eternity.

Oh most cruel serpent, infamous devourer, from its holy abode, the Word of God the Father, whose name is Adonai, has descended and has come to Earth from heaven to save mankind and to drive you away, evil and vile spirit, accursed by God and by all the heavenly court. Even by means of us, his ministers (though we are unworthy), the Word of God torments and fulminates against you, making you fall in a horrible manner to the bottom of the abyss, for all the words I have said are smoldering coals that burn with terrible power you and your helpers; they are words that make the whole world tremble, and any kind of heavenly, Earthly, and infernal creature fears, obeys, and adores them, and is frightened on hearing them.

You instead, oh accursed spirit, always want to be rebellious against your Creator. Woe to you, oh accursed and most vile spirit: get back, oh disgraceful one, by the force of all the holy exorcisms uttered against you. It is hard for you to defy the spur, and to want to resist against Christ. The later you come out, the greater will be your torture, for you do not despise a man, but he who is the king of kings and the lord of sovereigns, and he who will come to judge the living and the dead, and you as well, traitor of peoples.

May the holy Trinity, Father, Son, and Holy Spirit, the true divine majesty, fulminate against you instantly, oh devil, and send you to the deepest place in hell, without your ever more returning to this servant of God.

Rise, Lord, my God, rise, Lord, in your wrath, rise and hear my prayer. My God, move your power and destroy it, annihilate it with your terrible force and immediately cast your lightning against it. Help me, Lord, come to my aid. Rise, Lord, rise, oh my glory. Come down from heaven and descend: if you touch it, it will be destroyed. Cast your arrows and it will be brought low; at once send a terrible stroke of lightning against it, my God, who sits above the cherubim and seraphim. I have sinned, Lord, my God, have pity on me. May your mercy be upon us, oh Lord, for in you we have placed our hopes.

Lord, God of my salvation, you are my hope and my refuge. Amen.

Here, the exorcist, making the sign of the cross on the body parts of the possessed person, shall recite the following prayer:

PRAYER

Oh holy Lord, almighty Father, eternal God, drive out, then, this devil from your creature, [name], from his head, from his hair, from the top of his head, from his forehead, from his eyes, from his tongue and from underneath his tongue, from his ears, from his nostrils, from his neck, from his jaws, from his teeth, from his throat, from his gums, from his mouth, from his palate, from his brain, from the folds of his brain, from his eyelashes, from his eyebrows, from his hair, from his feet, from his tibias, from his knees, from his legs, from his intimate parts, from his kidneys, from his sides, from his upper and lower intestines, from his femur, from his belly, from his stomach, from his heart, from his shoulders, from his back, from his chest, from his breast, from his arms, from his hands, from his fingernails, from his bones, from his nerves, from his veins, from his bone marrow, from his lungs, from the structure of his body parts, from all his joints, from all his body, inside and outside, from the five senses of his body and of his soul. May this devil no longer find any place in this creature, either inside or out, so that this person will be safe and sane, by invocation of the holy name of your only-begotten Son and by the invocation of the Holy Spirit who is co-eternal with the Father. You, then, oh almighty God, who deigned to create the body and soul of this creature, deign also to liberate all his body and his soul from unclean spirits, and give him salvation.

We ask you this in the name of our Lord, Jesus Christ, who is God, and who lives and reigns with you in the unity of the Holy Spirit, forever and ever. Amen.

SEVENTH EXORCISM

TERRIBLE AGAINST DEVILS
THAT OPPRESS HUMAN BODIES

After observing the rules given in the first exorcism, the exorcist prepares to carry out his function by crossing himself, saying:

In the name of the Fa✝ther, and of the S✝on, and of the Holy ✝ Spirit. Amen.

Then he approaches the possessed person and sprinkles him with holy water, saying:

By aspersion with this water, and with the help of God, may the evil spirit go out of you, [name], and may the strength of the Holy Spirit enter you and remain with you forever. Now the judgment of the world is made, now the prince of this world is driven out. In the name of the Fa✝ther, of the S✝on, and of the Holy ✝ Spirit. Amen.

Then, pointing with his finger to the body of Christ in a chalice or in the tabernacle, he says these words:

Here before you, evil spirit, here is found supreme pity, he who suffered the passion for our salvation. Now the prince of this world will be driven out. This is the body of he who was assumed by the body of the Virgin; who was hung upon the wood of the cross, who was laid in the tomb, who rose from the dead and ascended into heaven before the eyes of his disciples. By his majesty and by his terrible power, I command you, oh evil spirit, to come out of this creature of God, [name]: flee from him and never more dare to molest him. Amen.

Here, the exorcist says these prayers, while kneeling:

Our help is in the name of the Lord.

HE MADE HEAVEN AND EARTH.

Show us, Lord, your mercy.

AND GIVE US YOUR SALVATION.

Lord, hear my prayer.

AND MAY MY CRY REACH YOU.

The Lord be with you.

AND WITH YOUR SPIRIT.

PRAYER

God, almighty and eternal, who created heaven and Earth, the seas and everything contained in them, who shaped man from clay, save and liberate your servant [name] from these evil spirits, and from every power of the devil, so that all men will know how great is your mercy and your infinite power. You who live and reign forever and ever. Amen.

PRAYER

Lord Jesus Christ, Son of the living God, by your holy clemency and mercy liberate your servant [name] from all torpor and agitation of shades and evil spirits. God Sabaoth, God Immanuel, God Elohim, God Agla, free him by the prayers, merits, and intercession of the blessed Virgin Mary, your mother, and of all the saints; by the intercession of Saint Michael Archangel and of all the angels, of Saint John Baptist, of the holy apostles, Peter and Paul, Andrew, James, John, Thomas, James, Philip, Bartholomew, Matthew, Simon, Thaddeus, Barnabas, and all the saints of God. By the heavenly hosts, the cherubim and seraphim, who each day praise your mercy saying: Holy, holy, holy, the Lord God Sabaoth, be favorable to me, a sinner, oh Lord God, almighty Father, who desire the salvation of all men and want them to reach knowledge of the truth; accept my prayer, which I raise before your mercy by your servant, [name], tormented by the devil, and who turns to your mercy. By the same Lord of ours, Jesus Christ, who is God and lives and reigns with you in the unity of the Holy Spirit, forever and ever. Amen.

PRAYER

Lord, God of Abraham, Isaac, and Jacob, show today that you are the God of Israel, that I am your servant (though unworthy) and have done each thing according to your precepts. Answer my prayers, Lord, answer my prayers, so that this people will learn that you are the almighty God who converts hearts. Answer my prayers, I supplicate you, through your mercy, oh most sweet and high Creator. Amen.

Here, the exorcist rises from prayer and, laying his hands on the head of the possessed person, says:

May every power of the devil be extinguished in you, [name], by the laying on of our hands; or rather, by the invocation of all the holy angels, archangels, patriarchs, prophets, apostles, martyrs, confessors, virgins, and all the saints.

In the name of the Fa✝ther, of the S✝on, and of the Holy ✝ Spirit. Amen.

Reading from the Gospel according to Matthew (4:1–11):

Then Jesus was led by the Spirit out into the desert. . .

Then the exorcist says this prayer:

The Lord be with you.

AND WITH YOUR SPIRIT.

PRAYER

Visit, Lord, we pray, this abode and your creature, push away from him all the snares of the enemy; may all your holy angels, Michael, Gabriel, and Raphael, abide in him, and protect him in peace from unclean spirits, and may your blessing be forever upon us. Through Christ, our Lord. Amen.

Here, the exorcist begins to exorcise the devils found in the body of the possessed person, so that they will come out. But he must be careful not to respond to their words unless necessary, for they are astute, lying spirits and, with their words, they try to deceive and prevent the works of exorcists. They often vulgarly threaten ministers and command them, saying they do not want to be disturbed. With force and courage, the exorcist must pronounce the following exorcism.

EXORCISM

I exorcise you, ✝ accursed demons who are in this body, from whatever part of the world you come, and who have received from God and from his holy angels power over this creature of God, [name]; I exorcise you, powers of the air and infernal princes, all you diabolical spirits, in general and in particular, of whatever species, sent from the East and from every region of the Earth. I exorcise you by the power of God the Fa✝ther, by the wisdom of his S✝on, by the virtue of the Holy ✝ Spirit, according to the strength of the authority that I exercise in the name of our Lord, Jesus Christ, the crucified Nazarene, Son of God, that is, the most powerful Creator who, from nothing, created and made to exist you, me, and all the beings of the world. I order you no longer to have the power to lie, be, or abide in this creature of God, [name], but I force and order you, whether you wish it or not, to show me your names, leaving aside every deceit, trick, or falsity.

By the same authority and by the merits of the most blessed Virgin Mary and all the saints, I unbind this creature of God, [name], from all spirits, and I send them to the depths of the infernal abyss. Go then, accursed ones, into the eternal fire, prepared for you and for all your companions; if you are rebellious and contumacious and do not obey me, by the same authority and with this exorcism I call, force, and command with power all the demons who are your enemies, and all the princes of hell, and the infernal furies to come and afflict you in the name of Jesus with every torment; and finally, may they lead you to undergo in the abyss the punishment I have announced to you. May the most holy names of God forever bind you to hell: El, ✝ Elohim, ✝ Eloah, ✝ Sabaoth, ✝ Eserheie, ✝ Adonai, ✝ Jehovah, ✝ Yah, ✝ Tetragram, ✝ Shaddai, ✝ Messiah, ✝ Hagos, ✝ Ischyròs, ✝ ho Theòs, ✝ Athànatos, ✝ Soter, ✝ Immanuel, ✝ Agla,

✝ Jesus, who is Alpha and Omega, ✝ Beginning and End. ✝ May he cast you into the depths of the abyss and into the fires of hell, so that you will have no power to stay, abide, or reside in this creature of God and image of Christ, [name], and shall not have power either over this or other places, by virtue of the holy names I have just invoked. And may the archangel Michael chain you to the depths of the abyss, in the name of the Fa✝ther, of the S✝on, and of the Holy ✝ Spirit. Amen.

Beginning of the Gospel according to John (1:1–14):

In the beginning was the Word, and the Word. . .

PRAYER

Lord Jesus Christ, Son of the living God, my God, have pity on me, do not let my soul be lost with the impious ones, Elohim the strong, Elohim the clement, Lord of fearing, Lord of the heaven hosts, Lord of mercy, Lord of eternal life, Adonai, wondrous Lord, ineffable Lord, almighty Love, Shaddai, power that never disappears, you who see everything, goodness that saves and creates, Alpha and Omega. Most powerful God, highest and most merciful.

Lord, who wanted to be prayed to by sinners with offerings of praise and supplications, we humbly pray you to hear us and have pity on us. Liberate us, save us, even though we are unworthy, oh our Creator and redeemer, by your glory, magnificence and pity, by your holy and glorious name, which is above every name.

Oh Redeemer, who came into this world by being born without sin of the Virgin Mary, if you looked upon our sins, you would not answer our prayers, but we pray, come to the aid of your servant whom you have redeemed with your precious blood and save us, oh most merciful Father. Into your hands, I give up my spirit and my body, today, now, and forever, at each hour and at every moment. Keep watch over your servant, a poor sinner, and this creature of yours, [name], so that we may give you thanks in your Church. You who live and reign forever and ever. Amen.

EXORCISM

I exorcise you, ✝ oh unclean spirits, who come from the four parts of the Earth and to whom power has been given to harm this creature of God, [name]. I exorcise you, powers of the air and infernal princes, and all you diabolical spirits, in general and in particular, of whatever sort, sent from the West and from every region of the Earth. Again I exorcise you ✝ and I exhort you, demons and spirits whom I named before, and all others existing in any part of the world. I oblige you who are of the Earth and I bind up you who are of the heavens; I force you who are of the wind and I tie up you who are of the fire; I imprison you who are of the waters and of the most secret caverns. I command you who are in the mountain caves, you who are of the mountain tops and you who are of the abysses of hell, you who are in every place under the heavens, through the Fa✝ther, the S✝on, and the Holy ✝ Spirit, by the authority I exercise in the name of our Lord, Jesus Christ, the crucified Nazarene, Son of the true and living God, and of the most powerful Creator, who has created me and you, who has made every creature. I command you, then, to lie no longer, nor to harm or stop or stay in this creature of God, [name], but I condemn you with the verdict proffered by the most high Creator, and I force you, I order you, whether you wish it or not, leaving aside every deceit, trick, and falsity, to show and reveal your names to me; by the same sentence of condemnation, I relegate you to the depths of the abyss and to the eternal fires. Oh iniquitous devil, tell us, then, what is your name, and the name of your master.

Here, the exorcist will interrogate the devil concerning its name, its allies, and everything regarding the liberation of the possessed person. Then he proceeds with the exorcism he has already begun.

Go then, accursed ones, into the eternal fire that has been prepared for you and for your servants, and by these most great and holy names of God, I detach you from this body; and by the force of these words and of these names, I relegate you to the depths of the abyss and to the eternal fire: El, ✝ Elohim, ✝ Eloah, ✝ Sabaoth, ✝ Eserheie, ✝ Adonai, ✝ Jehovah, ✝ Yah, ✝ Tetragram, ✝ Shaddai, ✝ Messiah, ✝ Hagios, ✝ Ischyròs, ✝ ho Theòs, ✝ Athànatos, ✝ Soter, ✝ Immanuel, ✝ Agla, ✝ Jesus, ✝ who is Alpha and Omega, ✝ Beginning and End, ✝ Root of Jesse, lion of the tribe of Judah; he sends you to the depths of the abyss, and may you no longer have any power to lie, stop, remain, or live in this creature of God and image of Christ, [name], nor in this place or in any other, by the strength and in the strength of said names. May the angel Raphael bind you to the depths of the abyss, where you shall remain bound and tormented till the day of judgment. In the name of the Fa✝ther, of the S✝on, and of the Holy ✝ Spirit. Amen.

Reading of the Gospel according to Mark (16:14–20):

Lastly, he showed himself to the Eleven. . .

PRAYER

Almighty and eternal god, who in the beginning created all things from the void; all the creatures you have created obey you and every knee bends before you, in heaven, on Earth, and in hell: the angels, archangels, thrones, principalities, powers and dominions. In your hand, you enclose all things, you created Adam and Eve in your image and you drove to the depths of Tartar the angels of Satan because of their pride. I pray, therefore, and I supplicate you, God, Father almighty and most merciful, through Jesus Christ, your Son, who has power over all things, who sits at your right hand and will come to judge with fire the living, the dead, and the entire world, he who is Alpha and Omega, the First and the Last, the king of kings and the sovereign of sovereigns, El, Ischyròs, Messiah; by all these most holy names, I invoke and supplicate you, by the birth of Jesus Christ, by that same Jesus who bore the cross, by his baptism and his passion, by his resurrection and ascension, by the wounds of his body, by his death and burial, by his omnipotent and ineffable virtue, by the holy Sacrament that you gave to his apostles the day before he died, by the holy and undivided Trinity, by the blessed and glorious Virgin Mary, by the angels and archangels, the thrones, dominions, principalities, and powers, the hosts of cherubim and seraphim; by the patriarchs and prophets, by all the saints; by all the mysteries and sacrifices that are celebrated in your honor, by your most holy names, I adore you, I supplicate you, I bless you, and I pray that you will accept these invocations of mine, the exorcisms and all the words of my mouth that I can use, so that I will be granted dominion over the angels of Satan, who were driven out of heaven and deceive mankind, so that I can understand their language and force them to obey my commands, tying up their powers and driving them away. Instantly before me, may they humbly carry out my orders, each time and wherever I wish. In no way may they despise my voice, but may they obey me and my words today, now, and forever, wherever I wish; may they fear me through your pity and mercy, by which I supplicate and pray to you, oh Immanuel, by all your names, by all the saints, by all the angels and archangels, the powers and thrones, by Adonai, El, Jehovah, Agla, Shaddai, by the sacred Tetragram and by all the holy names that are written in this book. Give me the power to bend to my orders all the evil spirits who have invaded this creature of yours, [name]. Make them respond to my questions and allow me to force them to obey, mildly and humbly, without lesion, fear, or harm to my body or soul.

Father of heaven, one in substance, three in persons, who permitted the sin of Adam and Eve and the sins of many others; for their sins, you wanted your Son to be crucified and to suffer death; I pray you, oh most merciful God, I supplicate you and invoke you in every way, by Christ, your Son, who is Alpha and Omega, to help me to dominate and expel from this creature of yours, [name], these spirits and all the angels of Satan who were cast down from heaven. So that you will grant me this power, here, Lord, I praise you, I glorify you, and I worship you, while these wretched enemies of yours refuse to do so. I subject myself to you spontaneously, with joy, and I humbly offer you everything that is mine, or rather, yours, almighty God, against whom these arrogant spirits are rebellious, while I bless you forever and ever. Amen.

EXORCISM

I exorcise you, ✝ demons and unclean spirits come from the four corners of the world, which have received from God the power to harm this creature of his, [name]; I exorcise you, powers of the air and infernal princes, of whatever sort, sent from the southern lands and from any other region of the world, and all those who are found in this creature of God. I force you obey to my orders from the Earth, I bind you from the fire, from the winds, from the waters, from the rocky caverns; I command you from the mountains, from the abysses, from hell and all places under the heavens, through the Fa✝ther, the S✝on, and the Holy ✝ Spirit; by the authority that I exercise of our Lord, Jesus Christ, the crucified Nazarene, Son of God, the most powerful Creator, who, from the void, created me and you and all creatures, I remove from you any power to stay, stop, or live in this creature of God [name]; instead, I condemn you with the verdict proffered by the most high Creator, and I order you to manifest your names to us, leaving aside every deceit, trick, and falsity. By the same verdict of condemnation, I unleash you from this body and I send you into the infernal fires.

Go then, oh accursed ones, into the eternal fires, prepared for you and for your companions. By these most holy names of God and by their virtue, I relegate you to the depths of the abyss: El, † Elohim, † Eloah, † Sabaoth, † Eserheie, † Adonai, † Jehovah, † Yah, † holy Tetragram, † Shaddai, † Messiah, † Hagios, † Ischyròs, † ho Theòs, † Athànatos, † Soter, † Immanuel, † Agla, † Jesus † Christ, † Alpha and Omega, † Beginning and End. † By all these names, I send you to the depths of the abyss and I order you no longer to possess any power to stay in or occupy this creature of God, [name], or this place or other places. By the authority of he who sits on the throne and who has the power to judge with fire the living, the dead, and the entire world, I condemn you to burn forever in the eternal fire, and I bind you till the day of judgment. In the name of the Fa†ther, of the S†on, and of the Holy † Spirit. Amen.

Reading from the Gospel according to Luke (1:26–38):

In the sixth month, the angel Gabriel was sent by God to a town in Galilee called Nazareth, to a virgin betrothed to a man named Joseph, of the House of David, and the virgin's name was Mary. He went in and said to her, "Rejoice, you who enjoy God's favor! The Lord is with you." She was deeply disturbed by these words and asked herself what this greeting could mean, but the angel said to her, "Mary, do not be afraid; you have won God's favor.

Look! You are to conceive in your womb and bear a son, and you must name him Jesus. He will be great and will be called Son of the Most High. The Lord God will give him the throne of his ancestor David; he will rule over the House of Jacob for ever and his reign will have no end." Mary said to the angel, "But how can this come about, since I have no knowledge of man?" The angel answered, "The Holy Spirit will come upon you, and the power of the Most High will cover you with its shadow. And so the child will be holy and will be called Son of God. And I tell you this too: your cousin Elizabeth also, in her old age, has conceived a son, and she whom people called barren is now in her sixth month, *for nothing is impossible to God.*" Mary said, "You see before you the Lord's servant, let it happen to me as you have said."

The word of the Lord.

PRAISE TO YOU, OH CHRIST.

PRAYER

God, unconquered source of power and king of insuperable dominion, magnificent, triumphant, who defeats with your force not only the enemies of your glory, but also the adversaries of good; you who, in order to redeem mankind who had fallen because of the devil and his envy, you wanted your Word to become flesh in the undefiled Virgin Mary; we humbly supplicate your almighty pity, that you might deign to liberate from tyranny and diabolical vexation this servant of yours, [name], who fears, honors, and adores you. We ask you this through Jesus Christ, who will come to judge with fire the living and the dead and the entire world. Amen.

EXORCISM

I exorcise you ✝ and I drive you out, evil spirits, angels who pursue Christians, through the Fa✝ther, the S✝on, and the Holy ✝ Spirit, by the undivided Trinity, by the virginity of the most blessed Virgin Mary.

I exorcise you ✝ and I drive you out by the archangels Michael, Gabriel, and Raphael, by the heavenly hosts, by the throne of divine majesty, by the immaculate Lamb who descended from heaven and was born of the Virgin Mary, as the angel had announced; by the most holy names of almighty God: El, ✝ Elohim, ✝ Eloah, ✝ Sabaoth, ✝ Eserheie, ✝ Adonai, ✝ Yah, ✝ by the holy Tetragram, ✝ Shaddai, ✝ Messiah, ✝ Hagios, ✝ Ischyròs, ✝ ho Theòs, ✝ Athànatos, ✝ Soter, ✝ Immanuel, ✝ Agla, ✝ Jesus, ✝ Alpha and Omega, ✝ Beginning and End, ✝ by all these and the other most powerful names of our Lord, Jesus Christ, Son of almighty God, living and true, I confute you, oh spirits, driven out of heaven through your fault and sent away from the most high throne.

Again I exorcise you ✝ and I command you by the ineffable power of the Creator, by the four beasts that stand around the holy throne of divine majesty, by the angelic powers, by the angels and the archangels, the thrones, dominions, principalities, and powers, by the hosts of cherubim and seraphim, who each day incessantly acclaim, saying: Holy, holy, holy, Lord God Sabaoth; by all this, I order you to get away from this creature of God and image of Christ, so that you can no longer harm any creature of God, made in the image of Christ, as it has been commanded of you. In the name of the Fa✝ther, of the S✝on, and of the Holy ✝ Spirit. Amen.

Great and Terrible Reproof of Satan Taken from Prierio[1]

Miserable and iniquitous spirit, here now, against you, I have invoked your Creator, he who will punish you, for you cannot continue without punishment impudently to scorn his generosity. You should have remembered how immediately, right from the beginning of your condition, he has justly scrutinized you. Hear, oh miserable one, your wretchedness.

God almighty, Adonai, great and wondrous, or rather, incomprehensible, being goodness and infinite love, needing nothing, but being in himself full of supreme felicity; yet by his infinite goodness, he wanted to create the universe, certainly to his glory, but also for the utility of others. For the good of creatures, he arranged for his glory to be manifest, being most pure and infinite goodness. He wanted there to be rational creatures in the universe, with which he wanted to enter into friendship out of holy charity, and to whom he wanted to give, at last, the happiness of communion with him. Among these creatures, they believe, there was also your supreme lord of Acheron, that is, Lucifer. But you spirits, who are now similar to beasts, but who were once glorious, you were created by almighty God, furnished with sublime natural gifts and gifts of grace that were higher still. Yet, at the very moment when you came into existence, you behaved, not only ungratefully, but rebelliously against your Creator, breaking out into enormous pride, rancor, and hate. Oh enormous ingratitude! Oh unheard-of audacity! Oh crime that must be expiated in the eternal flames!

Hear, then, what your great and wondrous Creator says by the mouth of Isaiah about your prince and about each one of you, in the image of the prideful person of Nebuchadnezzar: "How did you come to fall from the heavens, Daystar, son of Dawn? How did you come to be thrown to the ground, conqueror of nations?" This means: How could there have been in you such great pride and iniquity as to fall from the heavens at once, plummeting from divine power? You who rose as "son of the dawn"—that is, in the beginning of your existence, as a most beautiful morning star—you began to shine over the world; and yet you fell to Earth—that is, into hell, full of sulfur. You who governed peoples—that is, you were like a tyrant that thirsted for power, and exercised your rule over other spirits, you fell. You fell, I repeat, because you glorified your beauty and said in your heart: "I shall rise to the heavens," thus blaspheming your Creator, whereas you should have praised him. To rise into the heavens "over the stars of God" meant to want to reach eternal happiness with your own forces, and exalt your throne over all the heavenly spirits. You wanted, then, to reign over the other angelic spirits in a gratuitous, happy existence. "I shall live on the mount of the assembly," you said—that is, in the Jerusalem of heaven; "in the farthest parts of the north"—that is, in the middle of the temple, or in the heavenly church, for in the Earthly Jerusalem, the temple was found north of Mount Zion. Again, you said: "I shall rise over the superior regions of the clouds"—that is, I shall surpass in dignity and power all the created spirits, and "I shall be like the Most High"—that is, almighty God, who is blessed for his own virtue, not for that of others, and fills with beatitude all the blessed spirits.

Oh words full of audacity, to which the great and wondrous Adonai must rightly respond. Oh most proud and ungrateful spirit, you will be cast into the deepest lake of hell, for nothing is more just than to humiliate the proud. Those who see you fallen from such great dignity, vexing human bodies, and hiding among intestines full of excrement, in beastly attitudes, combining pig snorts with female howling, will stare at you in astonishment, seeing how low you have fallen from a sublime height, and they will say: "Is this not by nature a human being? And yet he has become a beast out of his own perfidious will"; he is a hellish invader who disrupts the Earth, for, having lost charity and the hope of salvation, with his deceits he tries to attract mankind into his rebellion and to plotting against God. That gives rise to infinite evil and to all kinds of grief, to the extent that the entire universe has been deprived of divine knowledge because of this scabby beast, who wanted to be adored everywhere instead of leaving that to his Creator.

How can you stand, oh miserable one, what God almighty declares by the mouth of Ezekiel regarding the king of Tyre, who symbolizes your person and was trained by your example? You who once were a cherubim, and now are an invader, a beast, a serpent, a skinny, starving pig, an unclean creature, so wretched that reality always surpasses every word. You were a "model of perfection," that is, the being most similar to almighty God, full of wisdom, both natural and of grace; while now you are full of foolishness and, even more, of moral iniquity; you were perfect in beauty, that is, in grace, and you inhabited the delights of God's paradise, for you were blessed in spiritual hope and in the promise of holy charity. You were covered with every precious stone—that is, every angelic spirit was your ornament, for you were surrounded by the nine hosts of angels. You were decorated by rubies, topazes, and diamonds, the first hierarchy in triple order; by chrysolite, onyx, and beryl, the second; by saphires, carbuncles, and emeralds, the third. Gold also formed your ornaments: that is, you had a splendid, most beautiful nature, gifted with natural force, with intelligence and will, and, in these qualities, as in golden rings, the gems of the gifts of spiritual virtues were set. All this was prepared on the day when you were created, for there was no imperfection in you, no disorder and no stain. You were similar to a cherubim, that is, with the two wings of love and contemplation,

you protected and covered the ark of the holy of holies—
that is, the Lord Sabaoth, or the church of heaven. God set
you on his holy mountain—that is, in a sublime place of
the celestial temple. You walked amid stones of fire—that
is, amid the holy angels, burning with love for God; you
were perfect in your conduct—that is, in your works, when
you took the first step along your way. Though your action
was one alone as regards measure, yet it was multiple as
regards the spiritual powers involved—that is, knowledge
and love. Ever since you were created—that is, from the
first instant of your existence, you were perfect, but then
iniquity was found in you—that is, in the second instant of
your existence. As your commerce increased, you were
filled with violence and sins—that is, despite the multitude
of gifts received from nature and from grace, you were inti-
mately filled with iniquity, and you sinned irreparably
because of the godlike intelligence given you, and by the
inviolable justice by which you were established.
Therefore, I drove you off the holy mountain of God,
pride-swollen as you were, become similar to a beast. From
the heavenly empyrean, I have sunk you into infernal darkness and I have made you perish, oh cherubim, who once
were the protector amid the stones of fire, of whose company you made yourself unworthy. You have lost wisdom
(God is my witness), though, among light women and
necromancers, you glory in your wisdom. From the angel
that you were, you have become a scabby, deformed
beast.

Oh miserable one, of which no creature is more
impudent and wretched, how is it that, after such great
glory, you dare to appear and emit brutal, pig-like
snorts? Be ashamed, oh disgraceful one, and flee,
respecting the commandments of almighty God. Indeed,
though an unworthy priest and servant of Jesus Christ,
the crucified Nazarene, by authority and with the power
of almighty God, Father, Son, and Holy Spirit, I order

you to occupy this temple of God no longer. Do not say, on the day of judgment, "No one drove me out, no one contradicted me." Here, oh vile gallows-bird, although I am an unworthy priest of almighty God and Christ, I contradict you, I order you to flee and invoke against you as witnesses and instruments of punishment, heaven and Earth; against you, I invoke the Holy Trinity, which will take revenge against your contumacy, and the blessed Virgin Mary; all the choirs of the good spirits; all the chosen of God to whom I humbly pray so that they will assist me against you. The legions of Tartar, instead, I shall certainly not invoke (far from me to do so, for, with the support of divine grace, I believe myself to be stronger than all the hosts of hell, both singularly and all together); instead, I convoke them, I cite them, I exorcise them on behalf of almighty God and I order them to punish your contumacy. Flee, oh miserable one, flee, oh thief, for the judge is coming in his wrath; the grievous and cruel torturer is coming in haste to hang you from the gallows of the infernal scaffold, as you are a thief and a robber. Here now, the judgment of Jesus Christ, the crucified Nazarene, is coming upon you; he will judge with fire the living, the dead, and the entire world. Amen.

Here, the priest places the book on the head of the possessed person, and showing him the crucifix, shall say:

> By the prayers and exorcism of this book, by all their virtue, by the miracles and words of our Savior, Jesus Christ, by all the prayers that are said in heaven and Earth, by all the heavenly hosts, by the power and force of the holy names of God, I order you not to need or be able to remain here any longer, but to do everything I shall command; otherwise, I will cast you down into the pool of fire and sulfur, to burn eternally. In whatever part of this body you

are, whether inside or out, come and see the sign of
the holy cross, ✝ consecrated by the supreme
Creator and our Lord, Jesus Christ; by his power,
you are obliged to obey me.

By this cross, I force you to come before me
against all your will. The words of God that come
out of my mouth are burning coals that will burn
you eternally. This is the sign of the cross, before
which all the world trembles and every creature is
frightened, while you are rebellious against our and
your Creator.

Now then, accursed ones, excommunicated and
blaspheming, may you be condemned to eternal
punishment; have no peace at any hour, unless you
immediately obey the commands I have made in the
name of Jesus Christ and the words that are said of
he who makes the world tremble. In his name, by his
power and virtue, I command you to go back immediately. Through Christ, who will come to judge
with fire the living, the dead, and the entire world.
Amen.

Sentence the Exorcist Must Pronounce against the Demons Tormenting the Possessed Person

Since in this judgment, I am a vicar of the supreme Judge,
by the power granted me by him, when he said to the disciples: "Everything you bind on Earth, will be bound in
heaven," after invoking his name and that of the blessed
Virgin Mary, his mother, as well as the blessed confessors
Prosperus, Geminianus, and Zenone, the holy martyrs
Justin and Ciprianus, and all the celestial court, ratifying
and approving the sentence already proffered by the
supreme Creator, as his vicar, I pronounce it, as I said
before, I declare it and I command you to restore to this

creature the health he had previously, no longer molesting him, withdrawing immediately, with no delay, and without creating any excuses.

Again I command, order, and impose against Lucifer, Beelzebul, and Satan, and all the infernal furies, by the authority given me, that they immediately cast you down into the pool of fire and sulfur, into the depths of hell, as was decided above; may they bind you there with no exception, and may they torment you with all the punishments till the day of judgment, for you were rebellious against your Creator, us, and his orders, those of the blessed Virgin, the teachings of the apostles, of the evangelists, the martyrs, and all the confessors. You have neglected the prayers and readings that we have done, and, therefore, I condemn you all to infernal punishment. May a fire issue from the very presence of God that will burn you and consume you by order of he who, with the Father and the Holy Spirit, lives and reigns forever and ever. Amen.

Here, the exorcist shall again show the crucifix to the devil, ordering him to come out by virtue of the names of God and of the cross; if the spirit should claim that he cannot come out, being tied to the possessed person by spells or exorcisms or other bonds, then the following formula of exorcism shall be used.

Liberation from Demons by Work of the Exorcist

I drive you out, † I contest you, and I exorcise you, and with this exorcism, I untie you, † accursed spirits, who are bound to this creature of God, [name], by force of all the miracles, graces, and powers of God and of this holy image of the Crucifix. By all the exorcisms, prayers, and exhortations, with which in the name of our Lord, Jesus

Christ, you can be condemned, forced to obey, afflicted by punishment; by the power and grace of God, by the tremendous day of judgment, when all of you are eternally tied down in the deepest abyss and in the pool of fire and eternal sulfur, I command you, oh rebels against Jesus Christ, the Nazarene, to come out and get away from this human body without doing any harm or physical or spiritual lesion, by virtue of the living and true God, in the name of the Fa✝ther, of the S✝on, and of the Holy ✝ Spirit. Amen.

The exorcist can demand the following promise from the demon tormenting the body, and this may be done in the place that seems most suitable to these exorcisms. He shall try to obtain the truth with harsh threats and severe orders.

Promise of the Devil that the Exorcists Must Demand in order to Tear the Truth from Him about Everything Regarding the Liberation of the Possessed Person

I promise you, priest, that is, minister of Christ, to observe everything that you order of me on behalf of God and of our Lord, Jesus Christ, the crucified Nazarene, and everything that regards his honor and the liberation of this creature, or else charity toward one's neighbor.

If I fail to do anything that I have promised you, from now on, I invoke against myself the same almighty God who in his wrath, as vindicator and guarantor of this promise of mine, shall send his holy angels, powerful in battle, to drive me away and expel me from this body.

In like manner, I call Lucifer, together with all the other princes, furies, and infernal punishments, so that they will rise against me in their indignation and furor and lead me to the deepest, most painful place in hell, where I shall be tormented a thousand times more atrociously and harshly than usual, with every pain, punishment, and infernal torture, from which I cannot be liberated forever and ever. Amen.

Since it often happens that demoniacs cannot be liberated from the unclean spirits who torment them in one, two or three instances, the priest who wants to put an end to the exorcism shall give this command to the spirits who have come out of the body.

Precept to be Imposed on All the Unclean Spirits Who Have Come Out of the Body of the Possessed

I order all of you, unclean spirits, who have come out of this body, in the name of the most holy Trinity, Fa✝ther, S✝on, and Holy ✝ Spirit, no longer to have any authority or power or possibility of showing yourselves to this creature of God, [name], or of making him perceive any illusion, real or fantastic. May you no longer be able to offend or injure him in body or soul, and may it not be granted you to return to him any more to vex him, nor send other demons in your stead.

By virtue of my precept, may you instead be forced to go into the darkness of hell, or into the places that God has destined for you, where you will have no way of harming any creature, whether rational or irrational.

Here is the cross ✝ of the Lord; flee, enemy forces. The lion of the tribe of Judah has won, the holy root of David is victorious.

If the demoniac is not yet liberated and yet it is necessary to terminate the exorcism, then all the spirits remaining in the body will be ordered and forced to get out of the head, the heart, and the stomach, and descend into the lower parts of the body, such as the dead toenails. Care must be taken not to allow them to remain in the upper parts of the body; when they have descended, the following order shall be given.

Precept to be Imposed on All the Spirits Remaining in the Body When There Is Need to Terminate the Exorcism

I order you, unclean spirits who are in this body, in the name of the most holy Trinity, Fa✝ther, S✝on, and Holy ✝ Spirit, subject to the punishment of being immersed in the pool of fire and sulfur for a thousand years after your exit, to have no authority or power to rise within the head or within the other members of this creature of God, [name], nor to harm him in any manner; instead, may you be forced to remain below, till you are called by me or another exorcist, or till you are allowed by God to rise, to his own honor, for the salvation of this creature and to your confusion, or for the increase of your pain.

Allow this creature to pray, eat, drink, rest, and perform all those actions that are consistent with God's honor and the salvation of his soul.

And as Christ died and, descending to hell, said: "Open, oh princes, your gates and burst open, eternal gates, so that the king of glory can enter"; as he will bind to hell Lucifer and all his pride, so I, too, by the authority which invests me, bind you to the place assigned you. In the name of the Fa✝ther, of the S✝on, and of the Holy ✝ Spirit. Amen.

When a possessed person is liberated, the following hymn of thanksgiving is recited.

Thanksgiving For The
Liberation of A Demoniac

Te Deum

We praise you, God, we proclaim you Lord.
Oh eternal Father, all the Earth adores you.
To you, the angels sing with all the powers of heaven:
Holy, holy, holy, Lord God of the universe.
Heaven and Earth are full of your glory.
The choir of the apostles acclaims you
With the white host of martyrs;
The voices of prophets join in your praise;
The holy Church proclaims your glory here on Earth.
Father of immense majesty,
We adore you, together with your only Son and the
     Holy Spirit paraclete.
You are the king of glory, oh Christ,
Eternal Son of the Father.
For the liberation of mankind, you were born of the
     Virgin,
Conqueror over death,
You opened to believers
The kingdom of heaven.
You sit at the right hand of God, in the glory of the
     Father.
You will come to judge the world at the end of time.
Help your children, oh Lord,
Who were redeemed with your precious blood.
Accept us in your eternal glory, in the assembly of
     the saints.
Save your people, Lord, bless your inheritance,
Guide and protect your children.
Each day, we bless you and praise your name forever.
Deign today, Lord, to protect us without sin;
May your mercy be always upon us,
For in you, we have hope.

Pity on us, Lord, pity on us.
In you, I have hope, Lord, I shall not be confused
    forever.

After the hymn, the following prayers are said:

Confirm, oh God, what you have wrought in us.

FROM YOUR HOLY TEMPLE, WHICH IS IN JERUSALEM.

Show us, Lord, your mercy.

AND GIVE US YOUR SALVATION.

Lord, hear my prayer.

AND MAY MY CRY REACH YOU.

The Lord be with you.

AND WITH YOUR SPIRIT.

PRAYER

We offer you thanks, holy Lord, almighty Father, eternal
God; we thank you, oh Christ, eternal Word of the Father;
we thank you, Holy Spirit, who sustains us. We give thanks
to all the saints, the angels, and men, for, thanks to the
power of God, through our hands the infernal dragon has
been defeated.

God of Abraham, God of Isaac, God of Jacob, have pity
on your servant, [name], whom you have freed from diabolical dominion, and, in his aid, make the Archangel Michael
come and protect him, visit him, and defend him from all his
enemies. You who live and reign forever and ever. Amen.

PRAYER

Almighty and eternal God, who have liberated this servant
of yours, [name], from every torment of Satan and his

ministers, send upon him from the heaven your holy seven-form Spirit paraclete. Amen.

The Spirit of wisdom and intellect.

AMEN.

The Spirit of counsel and strength.

AMEN.

The Spirit of knowledge and pity.

AMEN.

Fill him with the spirit of your fear, and mark him as suitable with the seal of eternal life.

AMEN.

The Lord be with you.

AND WITH YOUR SPIRIT.

PRAYER

With all our hearts, we recognize your greatness, we praise you and bless you, giving you thanks, oh God, non-generated Father, only-begotten Son, and Holy Spirit paraclete, holy and undivided Trinity. By your power today, together with his allies, the devil has been confused, upset, flagellated, and finally expelled from this creature, [name], whom you have deigned to redeem through your only-begotten Son.

I, therefore, pray you, holy Lord, almighty Father, eternal God, holy Trinity, lone power and inseparable majesty, our almighty God, deign to protect and defend with your holy angels this creature of yours, [name], from every assault by Satan and his ministers. Infuse in him your holy blessing. Through Christ, our Lord. Amen.

Here is the cross ✝ of the Lord: flee enemy forces.

The lion of the tribe of Judah has won, the holy root of David, Jesus Christ, son of the most blessed Virgin Mary, salvation of the world. He is the Lord who said to his disciples: "In my name, you will chase out devils"; may he himself, then, fulfill your word and be favorable and merciful to you. And may this sign of the holy cross ✝ be a shield and defense for you against any snare of the devil. Amen.

PRAYER

May God sanctify you with the seal of his holy cross ✝, so that all your enemies will leave you. May Jesus Christ defend you, Son of the living God, with the sign of the holy ✝ cross. May God ✝ defend you from all evil, present and future, external and internal. I mark you with the seal of the holy cross ✝, so that God will liberate you from the persecution of the devil. Before the image of this cross, may the devils, your enemies, bend and flee from you. By the sign of this holy cross, ✝ may God liberate you from the dangers of the world and send his holy angels to protect you.

May the blessing of God the almighty Fa✝ther, S✝on, and Holy ✝ Spirit be upon you. May the blessing of Jesus ✝ Christ be upon you. May the power of the holy cross ✝ be upon you, within you, around you, before and behind you, in every part of you. May the benediction of the blessed Virgin Mary, mother of God, be upon you. May the blessing ✝ of the patriarchs, prophets, apostles, martyrs, confessors, virgins, and all the saints of God be upon you. Amen.

PRAYER

Saint Michael Archangel, defend in battle this creature, [name], so that he will not perish in the tremendous judgment. By the grace that you have merited, I pray, save him from all the dangers of body and soul, from all the snares of the devils, and protect him, so that the evil spirits cannot harm him, wherever he is. Through Jesus Christ, our Savior. Amen.

Here, the priest or exorcist, making the sign of the cross on the possessed person, shall say:

I put on your forehead the sign of our Lord, Jesus Christ ☩. I make the sign of the cross ☩ on your eyes, so that they will see the light of God. I make the sign of the cross ☩ on your ears, so they will listen to the words of God for your salvation. I make the sign of the cross ☩ on your nostrils, so that you can smell the delicate perfume of God. I make the sign of the cross ☩ on your heart, so that you will recognize your sins. I put on you the sign of God, ☩ Father almighty, Son, ☩ and Holy ☩ Spirit, so that it will heal you and keep you healthy always in your life, so that the devil will have no more power over you, nor in any part of you; instead, may the holy Trinity sustain and guide you to eternal life. Amen.

Here, he blesses him, saying:

May our Lord, Jesus Christ, bless you ☩ and keep you.

AMEN.

May the Lord show you his face and have pity on you.

AMEN.

May he turn his face toward you and may he give you peace.

AMEN.

May the peace and blessing of almighty God, Fa☩ther,

S✝on, and Holy ✝ Spirit, descend upon you and remain with you eternally.

AMEN.

Conclusion

In looking back at the different phases during which Christian doctrine developed over the centuries, we note that, from the earliest days, the Church was extremely attentive to the problem of the devil. Theology regarding the topic, influenced by Judaic and Greek elements, is largely based on the Bible.

In the Christian tradition, demons and evil spirits are held to be creatures of God who rebelled against their creator, and tempted people to set themselves against the truth. The evil of demons is not inherent in their nature, which God created as good, but arose from their free choice. Some Church fathers declare that the fallen angels live between heaven and Earth. They cannot abide in heaven because of their sin; nor can they stay on Earth, which is reserved for man.

The punishment suffered by demonic beings is not definite: only with the universal judgment will their final destiny be known. Origen's view concerning the final conversion of the devil was not shared by many.

Most traditional authors believe that the devil's nature is spiritual, angelic; while some attribute subtle material elements to him.

The Church's harsh, open, face-to-face struggle against the devil was carried out through exorcisms whose invocations recall accounts in the gospel. Today, exorcism has become rare. In the Roman Catholic sphere, exorcists are few and far between, and normally operate only in large cities. Official Catholic theology tends to ignore Satan, and yet Vatican II affirmed: "The whole history of humanity is pervaded by a tremendous struggle against the forces of darkness, a struggle begun as soon as the world began." Among the common people, interest in Satan continues; indeed, it has intensified during the last few decades, as has an interest in magic, occultism, and even Satanic churches.

Some see in the "devil problem" a residue of the pre-scientific mentality; some, the expression of a negative presence insinuating itself into the life and history of the Church and mankind. For others, Satan is merely a symbol or an obsolete mythical figure. Karl Barth reduces him to a negative, non-real figure: the negativity of being.

More than one theologian doubts whether the Christian revelation means to attribute a real existence to the devil. Schoonenberg asks whether demons and Satan are mythical symbols; at any rate, he considers that they do not constitute an important part of the revelation. Some maintain that the devil acquires importance today because of the greater dimension of evil present in humankind. Even his presence in the New Testament is held to be metaphorical, the message being that Christ has conquered evil. Much of demonology involves this fantasy; even the liturgical formulas of the renunciation of Satan, and the exorcists' use of that same water, oil, and salt that are present in baptism, have an origin in pagan rites.

Some object, however, that Christ was "tempted by the devil." H. Haag holds that this affirmation was a device signifying that he was a true human. Temptation is part of the human condition: "We would not be normal, authentic men if we did not undergo any temptation."

There are still many theologians who believe differently; according to their interpretation of the Scriptures, denial of the real existence of devils is not licit. Paul VI and John Paul II have often taken up the topic, expressing their personal conviction that the revelation intends to teach that the presence of the devil is not mythical or symbolical, but personal and malignant.

Whatever each one of us may believe as individuals today, we seem to have come a long way from the frenetic, fascinated horror and rancor expressed by Girolamo Menghi. In its view of that mysterious, invisible being or non-being, humanity wavers between fear and the irritation one may feel for dry leaves, destined to be burnt or blown away by the cold wind of autumn.

APPENDIX

The following entries are drawn from chapters VIII and IX in the first part of Menghi's *Flagellum daemonum* respectively. However, while Menghi directly quotes the Scripture passages referenced, I shall simply indicate the point in the Old or New Testament at which the passage is found.

Explanation of several Hebrew and Greek names of God that are profusely used in the exorcisms.

The exorcist must take care not to adopt names that are unknown to him, for according to Saint Chrysostom, this is very dangerous. Since our collection of exorcisms contains many names which are unknown to the simple, but that are nonetheless most holy names of God, in order not to leave their spirits perplexed, I have decided to include an explanation of them at this point. Thus, each exorcist can safely use these prayers at his pleasure, with no hesitation.

One must note that, according to Saint Jerome in his letter to Marcellus (Book III, *Letters*), the first name of God is *El*, which the Septuagint interprets as *Powerful God*.

The second and third are *Elohim* and *Eloah*, which mean God himself.

The fourth name is *Sabaoth*, which the Septuagint translates as *God of Might*, and Aquila translates as *God of hosts*. The fifth name is *Elion*, which means "Most High." The sixth is *Eserheie*, as we read in Exodus; it means "he sent me." The seventh is *Adonai*, which we usually translate as "Lord." The eighth name is *Jah*, which is attributed only to God and is echoed in the last syllable of Hallelujah (praise God) as well. The ninth is the holy tetragram, which the Jews consider ineffable, that is *Jahveh* (Jehovah). The tenth is *El-Shaddai*, which, among the Jews means "God of Heaven," according to the Aquila translation; we can interpret it as "powerful God, capable of doing anything." All these names are explained by Jerome in the passage mentioned above.

But there are many other names of God that are unknown; some reject these names as superstitious and deserving of condemnation. However, if we consider them with care, we realize that they are holy names. They include: *Hagios, ho Theos, Ischyros, Athànatos.* In his treatise *De Sortilegiis*, Paolo Ghirlando says he extorted these names from evil sorcerers, and he claims that they have the equivalent meaning of *Acharon*, or immortal God. Now, in his opinion, *Acharon* is the name of Satan, or Beelzebub.

We can easily understand how far this explanation is from the truth by the fact that the Holy Roman Catholic Church uses these names on the day of the Parasceve (Good Friday) in order to supplicate God for the forgiveness of sins the world over. If they were vain, superstitious words, not only would the Church not use them, but it would surely condemn them. I am, therefore, amazed that such an honest, prudent, and erudite man as Ghirlando was not aware of this, since it is a fact known to everyone, especially to the faithful.

There are, then, other names, not known to everyone, that are utilized here and there, such as *Soter*, a Greek name meaning "savior" in our language. Among the Jews, *Jahveh* (Jehovah) is the great name of God that must not be pronounced; its interpretation can be read in the work of Galatino, *Conto gli ebrei*, and in the description of the name of Jesus made by Father Arcangelo Pozzo. *Agla*, too, is a Jewish name, one of the greatest; it means "You are the powerful God forever," as Galatino explains in his second book against the Jews, *De divinis nominibus*. *Homousion* is a Greek name meaning "consubstantial." It is attributed to Christ, as he is of the same substance as the Father and the Holy Spirit. *Eheye* is a Hebrew name simply meaning the essence of the divinity of God, again according to the explanation given by Father Arcangelo Pozzo.

Explanation of several Latin names of God that the author uses here and there in various exorcisms.

In the exorcisms in this book, there are several names of God found in various passages of the Holy Scripture or derived from the holy doctors of the Church; but not everyone is capable of finding the passage from which they are taken. For this reason, I have indicated for each name the corresponding source, so that each exorcist, if he so wishes, can know it and use it with certainty.

Alpha, Omega, First, Beginning, End: These names are found in Apocalypse 1:8.

Messiah, Christ: So we read in John 4:25.

Jesus: Luke 2:21.

King: John 18:37. In its hymns and prayers, the Church very frequently uses the name "king": "Christ, most merciful king," "King and creator of time," "Lord, everlasting king," "When that most powerful king," "Eternal and most high King," "King of mankind," "King of martyrs."

Immanuel, Legislator: Isaiah 7:14. The Church sings this name in honor of Christ in the seventh major antiphony, in preparation for Christmas: "Oh Immanuel, our King and legislator."

Light: John 8:12.

Father: Matthew 6:9.

Teacher and Lord: John 13:13.

Beginning: John 8:25

Vulgate Image: II Colossians 1:25.

Door: John 10:7.

Way, Truth, and Life: John 14:6.

Prophet: Luke 7:16.

Rock: I Corinthians 10:4.

Vine: John 15:1.

Key: So he is called in Isaiah (22:22), Apocalypse (3:7), and by the Church in the fourth major antiphony.

Power: Luke 1:35.

Firstborn: Luke 2:7.

Lamb: Isaiah 16:1

Vulgate: again, Isaiah 53:7; Jeremiah 11:7, 51:40.

Sheep: Isaiah 53:7.

Bridegroom: Psalm 18:6.

Creator: Genesis 1:1; and the Church sings in its hymns: "God, creator of all things," "Come, Creator, Spirit," "Supreme creator of light."

Redeemer: Repeatedly, the Church sings: "Christ, redeemer of all men."

Shepherd: John 10:11.

Master: Luke 5:5.

Splendor, Substance: Hebrews 1:3; and the Church sings: "You light, you splendor of the Father," "To you, Christ, splendor of the Father."

Judge: II Timothy 4:8.

Wisdom: Proverbs 9:1; I Corinthians 1:30: and the Church sings of Christ in the first major antiphony: "Oh Wisdom, who came out of the mouth of the Most High."

Sun: Malachi 3:20. And in speaking of the Virgin Mary, the Church says: "from you came forth the Sun of righteousness."

Morning star: Apocalypse 22:16.

Flower: Isaiah 11:1.

Priest: "Christ the Lord is an everlasting priest," sings the Church.

Pontifex: Hebrews 5:6.

Love-Charity: I John 4:8. And the Church sings: "Lively spring, fire, love."

Only-begotten: John 3:16; I John 4:9.

Paraclete: John 14:26; and in its liturgy, the Church sings: "You who are called Paraclete."

Mediator: I Timothy 2:5.

God, eternal, almighty: The Church uses these names with great frequency.

Power: I Corinthians 1:24; I Corinthians 1:18.

Bread: John 6:48.

Salvation: The Church sings: "You have come, you who are the salvation of the world.

Lion: Apocalypse 5:5.

Light: Luke 2:32.

Mouth: Isaiah 25:8.

Word: John 1:1; John 1:14.

Holy: Isaiah 6:3.

Almighty: Apocalypse 4:8.

Merciful: Exodus 34:6; Isaiah 54:10; Jonas 4:2; James 5:11.

Immortal: I Timothy 1:17; and the Church sings: "Holy, mighty, and immortal."

Peaceful King: As the church says in its liturgy: "The king of peace has been glorified."

East: So sings the Church in the fifth major antiphony: "Oh Sun of justice, who rises in the east like the splendor of eternal light."

Goodness: The Church says in its liturgy: "Oh Christ, true light, goodness, and life."

Supreme good: This is expressed in Pier Lombardo's *Magister sententiarum*, Book II, Distinction 1: "God made the creature rational so that it would understand the supreme good; and in understanding it, love it; and in loving it, possess it; and in possessing it, enjoy it."

Hope: Job 5:8,16; Psalm 13:6; Psalm 90:2 and 141:6

Vulgate Honor: the Church says, in the Office of the Trinity: "Oh our hope, our honor, blessed Trinity."

Spirit: John 4:24.

Guide: Thus the Church sings of Christ in the second major antiphony: "Oh Adonai and guide of the house of Israel."

Glory: Exodus 16:10; Psalm 3:4.

Mountain: As the Church says in one of its prayers: "Let us reach the mountain that is Christ."

NOTES

Preface

1. St. John Chrysostum, *De diabolo tentatore*, Homily 2, vol. 49, col. 257 of *Patrologiae cursus completus*, series graeca. (Paris, 1857–1866).
2. Giovanni Franzoni, *Il diavolo mio fratello* (Cosenza, 1986).
3. St. Ignatius of Antioch, *Epistola ad Romanos* in *Patres apostolici*. (Tubingen: Bihlmeyer, 1956), parts 5, 6.

Chapter 1

1. Ida Magli, *Sulla dignità della donna*. (Parma: Guanda, 1993). English title, unpublished: *Reluctant Lambs*.
2. Ireneus, *Controle eresie*, bk. III, no. 1; bk. V, no. 2.3 (Milan: Jaca Book, 1981).
3. Tertullian, *Adversus Marcionem*, vol. 2 of *Patrologiae cursus completus*, series latina (Paris, 1841–1864).
4. Tertullian, *De pudicitia*, vol. 19 of *Patrologiae*, series latina.
5. Tertullian, *De Baptismo*, vol 2 of *Patrologiae*, series latina.
6. Origen, *In Exodum homilia*, vol. 6, col. 3 of *Patrologiae cursus completus*, series graeca (Paris, 1857–1866).
7. St. Cyprian, *De Ecclesiae unitate*, vol. 3 of *Corpus scriptorum ecclesiasticorum latinorum* (Vienna, 1865), 207–233.
8. St. Cyprian, *Ad Donatum* (Vienna: Hartel, 1868), 5.
9. St. Clement of Alexandria, *Pedagogus*, bk. 1, no. 13 (Paris: Marrou-Harl, 1960–65).
10. St. Clement of Alexandria, *Protrepticon*, bk. 11, no. 4 (Paris: Mondesert, 1949).

11. Origen, *Commentarius in Joannem*, vol. 2. of *Patrologiae*, series graeca.

12. Origen, *Commentarius in Joannem*, vol. 2, cols. 13, 97 of *Patrologiae*, series graeca.

13. Origen, *De principiis*, vols. 1, 6, 3, cols. 408–409 of *Patrologiae*, series graeca.

14. Lactantius, *Divine Institues*, bks. I-VII, trans. Mary Francis McDonald (Washington: Catholic University Press, 1964).

15. Eusebius of Caesarea, *Preparatio evangelica*, in *Dimostrazione evangelica*, ed. P. Carrara (Milan: Paoline, 2000).

16. Athanasius, *Oratio de incarnatione Verbi*, in *Contra gentes - De incarnatione Verbi* (Oxford: Thomson, 1971) 25.

17. St. John Chrysostom, vol. 94 of *Patrologiae*, series graeca.

18. St. John Chrysostom, *In Joannnem*, vol. 16, col. 4 of *Patrologiae*, series graeca.

19. St. Ambrose, *Expositio Evangelii secundum Lucam*, vol. 4, col. 67 of *Patrologiae*, series latina.

20. St. Augustine, *De civitate Dei*, pt. 21, ch. 3, no. 1 (Madrid: Moran, 1958).

21. St. Augustine, *Sermones*, vol. 38, col. 1092 of *Patrologiae*, series latina.

22. St. Augustine, *De Trinitate*, pts. 13, 16, 20 (Rome: Sciacca, 1973).

23. Cassian, *Collationes*, vol. 7, col. 32 of *Patrologiae*, series latina.

24. St. Gregory the Great, *Moralia*, bk. 3, nos. 16, 34 (Paris: Turnhout, 1979).

25. St. Isidor, *Sententiarum libri tres*, vol. 83, cols. 537–738 of *Patrologiae*, series latina.

26. St. Maximus, *Capita quinquies cent*, vol. 90, cols. 1177–1392 of *Patrologiae*, series graeca.

27. St. John Damascene, *De fide orthodoxa*, vol. 94, cols. 873–877 of *Patrologiae*, series graeca.

28. St. Bruno, *Expositio in Epistolam ad Ephesinos, ad*

Romanos, ad Corinthios, vol. 153, col. 6 of *Patrologiae, series latina.*

29. Ibid.
30. Hildebert of Le Mans, *Sermones,* vol. 49, cols. 171, 582 of *Patrologiae,* series latina.
31. Brunone d'Asti, *Sententiae,* vol. 3, col. 65; vol. 8, cols. 964C-966B of *Patrologiae,* series latina.
32. Honoré d'Autun, *Elucidarium,* vol. 172, cols. 1114–1115 of *Patrologiae,* series latina.
33. Rupert of Deutz, *De victoria verbi Dei,* vol. 169, cols. 1121–1240 of *Patrologiae,* series latina.
34. St. Anselm, *Cur Deus Homo?* in *Obras completas de S. Anselmo* (Madrid: Schmidt, 1952), 2, 21.
35. Abelard, *Sic et non,* vol. 178, cols. 1405–1426 of *Patrologiae,* series latina. See also *Scito te ipsum,* vol. 178, col. 644B of *Patrologiae,* series latina.
36. *Summa Theologiae,* vol. 3 (Rome: Caramello, 1952).
37. *Scriptum super sententiis* (Paris: Moos, 1956).
38. John Paul II, *Insegnamenti di Giovanni Paolo II,* vol. IX 2, no. 284 (Rome: Poliglotta Vaticana, 1986).
39. Ibid., no. 282.
40. Daniel Pickering Walker, *Unclean Spirits: Possession and Exorcism in France and England in the Late Sixteenth and Early Seventeenth Centuries. (*London: Scholar Press, 1981).
41. In his *Flagellum daemonum, seu exorcismi terribiles, potentissimi, et efficaces in malignos spiritus effugandos de obsessis corporibus, cum sui benedictionibus, et omnibus requisitis ad eorum expulsionem.* Auctore R.P.F. Hieronimo Mengo vitallianensi ordinis Minorum regularis observantiae nuper in lucem proditum. (Venice: Domenico Malduram, 1576).
42. "Rituale Romanum, Pauli V Pontificis Maximi iussu editum, Romae 1614."
43. Pico della Mirandola, "Epistolae" in *Il Quattrocento* (Bologna: Zanichelli, 1966), 888–889.

44. B.L. Ullman, ed., *Coluccio Salutati, de saeculo et religione* (Pisa: Scuola Normale di Pisa, 1958).

45. Machiavelli, Niccolo, "Discoursi" in *Opere* (Milan: Zenit, 1966), 157.

46. Compendio dell'arte essorcistica et possibilità et stupende operationi delli Demoni et dei malefici con li remedij opportuni all'infirmitad maleficiali, di P.F. Girolamo Menghi da Viadana, Minore osservante." I consulted Giorno delle Sacre Stimmate del Beato Francesco [...]. (Bologna: Giovanni Rossi, 1578).

47. Fustis daemonum, adiurationes formidabiles, potentissimas et efficaces in malignos spiritus fugandos de oppressis corporibus humanis, ex Sacrae Apocalypsis fonte, variisque sanctorum Patrum auctoritatibus haustas complectens. Auctore R.P.F. Hieronymo Mengo vitellianensi, Ordinis Minorum regularis observantiae. (Venice: Domenico Malduram, 1606).

48. *Compendio dell'arte essorcistica...* (Bologna: Giovanni Rossi, 1578), Prologue 49. Menghi, *Compendio*, p. 4. The author quotes the prologue to John 1:3.

Chapter 2

1. Giralomo Menghi, *Compendio dell'arte essorcistica...* (Bologna: Giovanni Rossi, 1578), Prologue, p. 9.

2. Menghi, *Compendio*, p. 10.

3. Menghi, *Compendio*, p. 11.

4. Menghi, *Compendio*, p. 12.

5. Menghi, *Compendio*, p. 12.

6. Menghi, *Compendio*, p. 15.

7. Menghi, *Compendio*, p. 16.

8. Menghi, *Compendio*, pp. 21–23.

9. Menghi, *Compendio*, p. 21.

10. "Prediche italiane ai Fiorentini," F. Cognasso, ed., in *Il Quattrocento.* (Bologna: Zanichelli, 1966), pp. 853–869.

11. Menghi, *Compendio*, p. 37.

12. Menghi, *Compendio*, p. 37.

13. Menghi, *Compendio*, p. 40.
14. Menghi, *Compendio*, p. 42.
15. Menghi, *Compendio*, p. 47.
16. Menghi, *Compendio*, p. 47.
17. Menghi, *Compendio*, p. 56.
18. Riccardo de Media Villa, *Distinctio* VIII, 2 (so quoted by Menghi in *Compendio*, p. 6).
19. Menghi, *Compendio*, p. 6.
20. Menghi, *Compendio*, p. 62.
21. Menghi, *Compendio*, p. 72.
22. Menghi, *Compendio*, p.75.
23. Menghi, *Compendio*, p. 76.
24. Menghi, *Compendio*, p. 76.
25. Menghi, *Compendio*, p. 77.
26. Menghi, *Compendio*, p. 87.
27. Menghi, *Compendio*, p. 85.
28. Menghi, *Compendio*, p. 85.
29. Menghi, *Compendio*, p. 87.
30. Menghi, *Compendio*, p. 88.
31. Menghi, *Compendio*, p. 89.
32. Menghi, *Compendio*, p. 146.
33. Menghi, *Compendio*, p. 283.
34. Zaccaria Visconti, *Complementum artis exorcisticae*, (Venice), 16, 58, 86.
35. Valerio Polidori, *Practica exorcistarum* (Padua, 1587).
36. Floriano Canale, *Del modo di conoscere e sanare i maleficiati* (Brescia, 1622), 49 sqq.
37. Franc. Maria de Capellis, *Circulus aureus seu breve compendium coerimoniarum et rituum* (Naples, 1670), 308 sqq.

Chapter 3.

1. *Flagellum daemonum, seu exorcismi terribiles, potentissimi, et efficaces in malignos spiritus effugandos de obsessis corporibus, cum sui benedictionibus, et omnibus requisitis ad eorum expulsionem.* Auctore R.P.F. Hieronimo Mengo vitallianensi ordinis Minorum regularis

observantiae nuper in lucem proditum. (Venice: Domenico Malduram, 1576), 2.

2. Menghi, *Flagellum daemonum,* p. 2.
3. Menghi, *Flagellum daemonum,* p. 3.
4. Menghi, *Flagellum daemonum,* p. 3.
5. Menghi, *Flagellum daemonum,* p. 1.
6. Menghi, *Flagellum daemonum,* p. 9.
7. Menghi, *Flagellum daemonum,* p. 12.
8. Menghi, *Flagellum daemonum,* p. 13.
9. Menghi, *Flagellum daemonum,* p. 15.
10. Menghi, *Flagellum daemonum,* p. 15.
11. Menghi, *Flagellum daemonum,* p. 16.
12. Menghi, *Flagellum daemonum,* p. 19.
13. Menghi, *Flagellum daemonum,* p. 31.
14. Menghi, *Flagellum daemonum* , p. 36.
15. Menghi, *Flagellum daemonum,* p. 38.
16. Menghi, *Flagellum daemonum,* p. 38.
17. Menghi, *Flagellum daemonum,* p. 44.
18. Menghi, *Flagellum daemonum,* p. 45.

First Exorcism
1. Hebrew word, *YHWH,* indicating the name of God as revealed to Moses.

Seventh Exorcism
1. Silvestro Prierias OP, 1456–1523, composed *De strigimagarum daemonun mirandis.*

BIBLIOGRAPHY

The most complete collections of the relevant ancient Christian literature are *Patrologiae cursus completus*, edited by J. P. Migne, in the two series: *Patrologia latina*, Paris, 1841–1864, 221 volumes, plus supplements edited by A. Hamman; and *Patrologia greca*, Paris, 1857–1866, 161 volumes. The Latin collection covers the period up to Innocence III, and the Greek, up to the 15th century. Another important collection is *Corpus scriptorum ecclesiasticorum latinorum* (CSEL), Vienna, 1865. These works are referenced below by volume.

Abelard. *Sic et non.* Vol. 178 of *Patrologiae cursus completus*, series latina. Paris, 1841–1864.

———. *Scito te ipsum*, 3. Vol. 178 of *Patrologiae cursus completus*, series latina. Paris, 1841–1864.

Ambrose. *Expositio Evangelii secundum Lucam.* Vol. 15 of *Patrologiae cursus completus*, series latina. Paris, 1841–1864.

Anselm. "De casu diaboli," in *Obras completas de S. Anselmo*. Madrid: Schmidt, 1952.

———. "Cur Deus homo?" in *Obras completas de S. Anselmo*. Madrid: Schmidt, 1952.

Athanasius. *Contra gentes - De incarnatione Verbi*. Oxford: Thomson, 1971.

Aubin, P. "Intériorité et extériorité dans le 'Moralia in Job,'" *Recherches de Science Religieuse*, 62 (1974).

Augustine. *Confessionum.* Libri XIII. Turin: Wangnereck, 1962.

———. *De Trinitate,* Rome: Sciacca, 1973.

————. *De civitate Dei (La ciudad de Dios)*. Madrid: Moran, 1958 .

Barth, K. *Kirchliche Dogmatic*. Zurich: Zollikon, 1950.

Brunone d'Asti. *Sententiae*. Vol. 165 of *Patrologiae cursus completus*, series latina. Paris, 1841–1864.

Bultmann, R. *Cristianesimo primitivo nel quodro delle religioni antiche*. Milan: Garzanti, 1964.

Cassian. *Collationes*. Vol. 49 of *Patrologiae cursus completus*, series latina. Paris, 1841–1864.

Chrysostom, John. *De diabolo tentatore*. Vol. 49 of *Patrologiae cursus completus*, series graeca. Paris, 1857–1866.

————.Vol 94 of *Patrologiae cursus completus*, series graeca. Paris, 1857–1866.

Clement of Alexandria. *Le pédagogue*. Paris: Marrou-Harl, 1960–65.

————. *Le protreptique*. Paris: Mondesert, 1949.

Crouzel, E. "L'apocatastasi in Origene," *Parola Spirito e Vita* 19 (1989).

Cyprian. *Ad Domatum*. Vienna: Hartel, 1868.

Damascene, John. *De fide orthodoxa*. Vol. 94 of *Patrologiae cursus completus*, series graeca. Paris, 1857–1866.

————. *De diabolo et daemonibus*. Vol. 94 of *Patrologiae cursus completus*, series graeca. Paris, 1857–1866.

D'Autun, Honoré. *Elucidarium. Liber duodecim quaestionibus*. Vol. 172 of *Patrologiae cursus* completus, series latina. Paris, 1841–1864.

Duquoc, C. "Symbole ou réalité?" *Lumière et Vie* 15 (1966).

Eusebius of Caesarea. *Praeparatio evangelica, in Dimostrazione evangelica*. Ed. P. Carrara. Milan: Paoline, 2000.

Flick, M., and Alszeghy, Z. "Gli angeli," *Il Creatore. L'inizio della salvezza*. Florence, 1964.

Gregory the Great. *Moralia in Job*. Paris: Turnhout, 1979.

Haag, H. "Das Bose oder Bose. Die Frage nach dem Reufel als Theologische Frage," *Zeitwende*, 46 (1975).

Hildebert of Le Mans. *Sermones; Tractatus theologicus.* Vol. 171 of *Patrologiae cursus completus*, series latina. Paris, 1841–1864.

Ireneus of Lyon. *Contro le eresie.* Milan: Jaca Book, 1981.

Isidor of Seville. *Sententiarum libri tres.* Vol. 83 of *Patrologiae cursus completus*, series latina. Paris, 1841–1864.

Kasper, W. "Die lehre der kirche von Bosen," *Stimmen der zeit*, 196 (1978).

Kelly, H. A. *The Devil: Demonology and Witchcraft.* London, 1968.

Lactantius. *Divine Institutes.* Bks. I-VII. Trans. Mary Francis McDonald. Washington: Catholic University Press, 1964.

Maximus. *Capita quinquies cent.* Centuria, 2, 67. Vol. 90 of *Patrologiae cursus completus*, series graeca. Paris, 1857–1866.

Menghi, G. *Flagellum daemonum.* Venice: Malduram, 1576.

————. *Fustis daemonum.* Venice: Malduram, 1606.

————. *Compendio dell'arte essorcistica.* Bologna: Giovanni Rossi, 1578. (1st ed. 1576.)

Moltmann, J. "Zwolf beverkungen zur symbolik des Bosen," *Evangeliche Theologie*, 52 (1992).

Mulder, D. C. "I demoni nelle religioni bibliche," Concilium, 10 (1975).

Origen. *De principiis.* Vols. 1, 6, 3, cols. 408–409 of *Patrologiae cursus completus*, series graeca. Paris, 1857–1866.

————. *Der Joanneskommentar.* Ed. E. Preuschen. In *Die Griechischen Christichen Schriftsteller, Origenes Werke IV.* Leipzig-Berlin, 1903.

Petrocchi, M. *Storia della spiritualità italiana.* Vol II. Rome: Edizioni di storia e letteratura, 1978.

Polidorus, V. *Practica exorcistarum.* 1st ed. Padua, 1587.

Ratzinger, J. "Liquidazione del diavolo?" *Dogma e predicazione.* Brescia: Morcelliana, 1974.

Ricoeur, P. *La symbolique du mal.* Paris: Seuil, 1968.

Rupert of Deutz. *De victoria verbi Dei; De glorificatione Trinitatis et processione Spiritus S.* Vol. 169 of

Patrologiae cursus completus, series latina. Paris, 1841–1864.

Schlier, H. *Machte und Gewalten im Neven Testament*. Basel, 1963.

Schnackenburg, R. *Il Vangelo di Giovanni*. Trans. Vincenzo Gatti. Brescia: Paideia, 1987.

Schoonenberg, P. et. al., "Osservazioni filosofiche e teologiche," in *Angeli e diavoli*. Brescia: Marcelliana, 1974.

Visconti Zaccaria. *Complementum artis exorcisticae*. Venice, 1600.

Walker, Daniel Pickering. *Unclean Spirit: Possession and Exorcism in France and England in the Late Sixteenth and Early Seventeenth Centuries*. London: Scholar Press, 1981.

Various authors. "Pourquoi choisir le diable?" *Choisir,* 179 (1974).

———."Teufel und Damonen," *Bibel und Kirche,* Quartal, 1975.

Werbbick, J. *Soteriologie*. Dusseldorf, 1990.